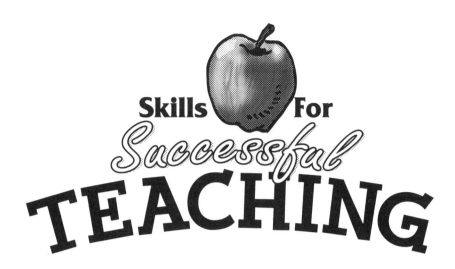

Skills For Successful TEACHING

By
**Barbara Allman,
Sara Freeman,
Jeffrey Owen,
Sally Palow,
and
Vicky Shiotsu**

Cover illustration by
Peter Thompson

Inside illustrations by
Marty Bucella

Icon illustrations by
Maria Marfia

Publisher
Instructional Fair • TS Denison
Grand Rapids, Michigan 49544

Instructional Fair · TS Denison

Skills For Successful Teaching
was previously published by Instructional Fair • TS Denison
under the Step-By-Step Series of titles:
Teaching Children Organization, Time Management, & Study Skills,
Teaching Children Conflict Resolution, Building Self-Esteem, Improving Writing Skills,
Planning a Great Science Fair Project, Teaching a Multi-Age Group, Making Current Events Meaningful,
A Teacher's Survival Guide, Kids as Curators: Museum Explorations,
Using Community Resources & People, Conducting a Successful Field Trip,
and *Teaching Multicultural Awareness.*

Credits

Authors: Barbara Allman, Sara Freeman,
    Jeffrey Owen, Sally Palow,
    and Vicky Shiotsu
Cover Artist: Peter Thompson
Inside Illustrations: Marty Bucella
Icon Illustrations: Maria Marfia
Project Director: Deborah Hanson McNiff
Editors: Debra Olson Pressnall and
    Karen Seberg
Cover Art Direction: Darcy Bell-Myers
Text Design: Deborah Hanson McNiff

About the Authors

Barbara Allman is an education writer and former teacher. She holds a Bachelor's degree and a Master's degree in Elementary Education from Oakland University. She has worked as a primary grade teacher and a K–6 reading specialist.

Sara Freeman grew up in Phoenix, Arizona, and taught elementary school in Tucson. She worked as an editor in Southern California, writing and editing educational products for children. She is now a freelance writer in Boulder, Colorado. Sara keeps current with educational methods by volunteering in elementary school classrooms.

Jeffrey Owen is a practicing clinical psychologist, author, and educator. Formerly a school psychologist, Jeffrey is now a special education consultant to several school districts in San Diego, California. He also conducts workshops to teach parents and teachers how to help children deal with interpersonal conflicts and other problems.

Sally Palow motivated children in the classroom for sixteen years before beginning her career as an educational writer and product developer. In addition to creating instructional materials, Sally regularly presents educational workshops to parents and teachers.

Vicky Shiotsu was an elementary school teacher in British Columbia for eight years. She now resides in Los Angeles, where she has worked as a tutor to Japanese students, a teacher at a Reading Center, and an editor for an educational publishing company. She is currently a free-lance writer and educational consultant.

Table of Contents

A Teacher's Survival Guide

Kids as Curators—Museum Explorations

Using Community Resources

Conducting a Successful Field Trip

Teaching Multicultural Awareness

Internet Information

Teaching Children
Organization, Time Management, & Study Skills

Introduce your students to the real satisfaction that comes from being organized and prepared for learning! This chapter contains tips and practical steps to help your students form good study habits. There are also strategies to encourage your students to make the most of their time and efforts. Included is a sample schedule and checklist, and ideas for assessing your students' progress.

Communication

ATTITUDE IS EVERYTHING

A positive attitude is a powerful tool that fosters enthusiasm, promotes self-esteem, and creates an atmosphere conducive to learning. If your students do not believe in themselves and their abilities, it is important to change that belief for learning to take place. You can nurture a positive learning attitude by verbalizing positive expectations and by expressing praise for jobs done well and on time. Try these tips for building positive attitudes:

• Show students that well-deserved self-praise is healthy by commenting aloud on your own performance. *Example:* "I like the way I read that story." Frequently mention the satisfaction you get from some work-related job you have done well.

• Look for opportunities to praise your students' efforts. Even a little recognition, as long as it is genuine, goes a long way. *Tip:* Avoid hollow praise—save words like "terrific" for truly outstanding accomplishments. Use a smile, a light touch on the shoulder, or a wink to recognize everyday efforts.

• Encourage your students to look upon their educations as their "jobs." But rather than working for someone else, they are working for themselves. Explain that they are building the foundation for their futures—each thing they learn is like a brick laid for a future skyscraper! What they do now can help them stand tall and strong throughout their lives.

- Encourage your students to develop an interest in what they are learning. Interest is a great aid to learning. Explain that the more they learn about a subject the more their interest will increase.

- Give your students positive reinforcement for desired behavior and attitudes.

- Set up a reward system for accomplishing short- and long-term goals. When used properly, rewards can be an effective way to bring about desired study habits.

- Let your students see how you organize yourself. Show them your lesson plans, your daily schedule, and other organizational tools you use. Ask them to speculate about what a school day would be like if there were no set plans for what to do and when.

- Make the tips you present on organization, time management, and study habits meaningful and relevant to your students. *Example:* As you give an in-class assignment, ask the students to estimate how long they think you should allow for completing it and why. Tell them how you estimate the time an assignment or other activity could take and how you rely on these skills daily.

- Show your students how you schedule your time and activities. Stress the importance of organizing one's time.

- Point out to your students that everyone is required to do tasks of which they are not particularly fond. Talk to them about some of the things you must do and how you motivate yourself to tackle them.

- Encourage your students to use "mind-motivators"—thoughts that get them mentally moving. Have them think about activities they must force themselves to do, such as homework or piano practice. Tell students to motivate themselves by applying "mind talk" to do these things. *Example:* "If I start this now, I'll be done before dinner, and still have time to go out and play!" Help them practice this technique—it works!

- Impress upon your students that they are in control of what they do. Tell them to visualize being the driver on the "bus of life," not a passenger.

Rule of Thumb

A good rule of thumb: You have two main responsibilities in helping your students form good study habits. One is to ensure that the subject is presented clearly and reinforced appropriately. The other is to teach your students how to study and learn on their own.

ORGANIZATION

Teaching organization, time management, and study skills should be as much a part of instruction as reading, math, and social studies. Your students will benefit from focused instruction that supports their learning efforts across the curriculum. Remember, they need your guidance and plenty of practice to develop good and consistent habits. Follow these steps:

Steps to Take

1. Create the best possible environment for study. *Tip:* Share these ideas with parents for setting up a study area at home.

   - Make sure the study area has good lighting, good ventilation, a comfortable chair, and a sturdy work surface.

   - Choose a quiet place to study.

- Study in the same place every day. This gets the mind in gear and helps concentration.
- Devote a desk or table only to studying. It should be large enough to spread out work and hold supplies.
- Remove items from the study area that may distract or interrupt concentration.

2. Make sure your students have all the supplies and materials they need to do their work and stay organized: pencils, pens, scissors, tape, glue, rulers, erasers, paper, a dictionary, and notebooks. Make a cardboard tray (cut from a box) to hold supplies, or label pockets of a hanging shoe holder for storing materials.

3. Establish a permanent work center in your learning environment. Make and post a fancy "Learning Zone" sign to identify the area.

- Create a message board in the Learning Zone where you and your students can exchange information. Students can use it to ask for help from you or another student, post messages, or display work. You can use it to post assignments.
- Supply the Learning Zone with color-coded folders for organizing work by subject or topic.

4. Instruct your students to keep notebooks that contains a supply of paper and all the work for each of their classes. Help them organize their notebooks by offering the following suggestions:

- Use dividers for each subject. *Tip:* If an instructor requires a separate notebook for each subject, dividers can still be used to separate sections or units. *Example:* Science notebook sections—class notes, homework, experiments, text notes.

- Put a zippered plastic bag in the front of the notebook to hold pencils, erasers, an assignment book, or other materials. *Tip:* If using spiral notebooks, carry supplies separately in a zippered bag or a pencil box.

- Keep a monthly calendar in the notebook. Record and circle the dates of upcoming tests, due dates of long-term projects, school activities, and extra-curricular activities. Check the calendar daily.

  Tip: Calendars are easy to create on a computer. One student can make a master calendar, then reproduce it for the whole group.

- Know where the notebook is at all times and keep it well-stocked. When an assignment is complete, put it safely in the notebook until it is time to hand it in. *Tip:* Do not put papers in between the pages of the books where they will be lost or forgotten.

5. Suggest that students use pocket folders for all returned assignments, tests, etc. *Tip:* Plain pocket folders can be color-coded by subject. Remind students to keep returned papers for a reasonable length of time—at least until the end of the grading period. If any questions arise about a grade or a missing assignment, the mystery can be solved by consulting the returned papers folder.

6. Help your students learn to keep track of assignments. Every time you give homework assignments, announce tests, and assign book reports or projects, make sure your students record the assignments. If they do this repeatedly, it will become a habit.

Ideas

7. Generate excitement about getting organized by distributing a gift to each student. Purchase inexpensive assignment books, or make your own assignment sheets and fasten them together in book form. Gift wrap the books and place them in a basket. Train students to write all assignments in their books. Check their assignment books on a weekly basis the first month of class.

SAMPLE ASSIGNMENT SHEET

Name: _____

Date: _____

Subject: _____

Assignment: _____

_____

Date assigned: _____

Date due: _____

Did I estimate the time I needed correctly? _____

Did I proofread my completed work? _____

Did I use my time well? _____

How could I have worked more efficiently? _____

_____

TIME MANAGEMENT TECHNIQUES

Ideas

Have you ever wondered how you were going to get everything accomplished in the time available? Your students experience the same problem. The solution does not lie in finding more hours in the day but in using time more efficiently. Try these time-management techniques with your students:

• Instruct your students to track how they spend their time for two full days. Realizing how they spend their time will make your students better time managers. Follow up by asking them to evaluate their use of time in the 48-hour period. *Example:* spend time in such a way that you accomplish what you need to do and still have time for things you like to do?

• Use a timer in your learning environment to encourage students to work within time limits. This is especially helpful for students who are capable but lack self-discipline with regard to time use.

Tip: Invite students to use the timer in the Learning Zone and to try the same technique in their study areas at home.

• Instruct the students to make a study or practice schedule and stick to it.

Rule of Thumb

A good rule of thumb: Management tools such as schedules, checklists, and contracts motivate students and allow them track their own progress.

- Prevent daydreaming. Call a "time to think break." After a moment or two, snap your fingers to signal that it is time to tackle the work again. Your students can self-direct their study time using this technique.

- Teach your students to rely on daily lists, crossing off tasks they complete throughout the day. *Example:* Things To Do Today—Remember lunch money, turn in homework, clean the gerbil cage, get to soccer practice by 4:00, study, write Grandmother a thank-you note.

- Tell your students to attach permanent time-saving checklists to their work areas with any reminders they need frequently. *Example:* Did I put my name on my paper? Did I write down my assignments?

- Conduct an end-of-the-week chat with your students. Review their activities  that week, and ask them to check their lists and assignment notebooks to review what they accomplished. If they did not get everything done, ask them how they can improve the next week. Establishing the habit of a weekly review will help teach them to evaluate their priorities.

Suggestions

- Teach your students to tackle tasks in manageable chunks. This will help keep them from viewing their workloads as overwhelming.

- Point out to your students that they can reduce stress on long-term projects by anticipating and planning for deadlines well in advance. This serves the dual purpose of ensuring enough time to complete the assignment and allowing for review and revision of their work.

- Support your students if they are having difficulty getting their assignments done and managing time. Create work contracts with them and reward them for reaching short-term milestones. This develops great work habits and leads to more competent long-term time planning.

A good rule of thumb: Keep students from feeling overwhelmed by the many time-related issues they face each day. Instruct them to set short, easily attainable time and work goals and to note their successes in accomplishing their tasks. Keep telling them, "Inch by inch, it's a cinch."

Rule of Thumb

Steps to Take

- Share these six time management techniques with your students:

1. Study difficult subjects *first*. If math is hardest for you, do it first. If you put these subjects off to do later, they may never get done.

2. Determine your best time to study. Some students study best when they first get home from school. Others do better after dinner. Some even like to get up early in the morning. Try studying at different hours to discover your best learning time.

3. Turn off the television, radio, and stereo when you study. You may not like it, but the vast majority of research shows that silence is the best music for your study time.

4. Hang a "Do Not Disturb" sign on the door of your study area when you are working. (Discuss this with family members first.) You will save lots of time if you are not interrupted while you study.

5. Stay off the phone during your study time. Tell someone in your family to take messages for you.

6. Do not get too relaxed! Study where you will be comfortable, but not so comfortable that you get sleepy.

STUDY SKILLS STRATEGIES

Communication

You can help your students organize themselves for learning by developing their listening and preparation skills. Begin by teaching your students the following listening techniques:

- **Listen for numbers** that tell what assigned pages to read, problems to do, length of a report, etc.
- **Listen for key words**—important words that tell you to do something, such as read, work, study, draw, circle, tell, decide, remember, underline, choose, fill-in.
- **Important words** are often repeated or emphasized.
- **Picture directions in your mind.** *Example:* Circle the correct answer.
- **Write down direction notes** in your assignment notebook.
- **Look for nonverbal clues,** such as gestures or changes in voice, that are used to emphasize important points.
- **Finish listening before drawing conclusions.** Let the person finish speaking, then evaluate what you heard.
- **Ask yourself** if you understand what was said.

Listening is a prerequisite for acquiring basic study skills, such as understanding assignments, managing time, and taking notes. Your students spend more time in their learning environment listening than doing any other single activity. Help them "tune in" with these ideas.

- Instruct your students to assume a listening posture when you are ready to give directions. You might have them fold their hands and look at you. Tell them that when you say, "Let's listen," you want them to assume this posture.
- Ask your students to respond to a series of questions that require careful listening. *Example:* Read a paragraph, then ask questions about what you read.
- Poor listening habits often stem from students' assumption that directions will be repeated. Tell your students that you will give directions only once.

Students in the middle grades and above must cope with greater organizational demands—changing classes, using lockers, keeping notebooks and folders for each class, and remembering assignments and homework given by multiple teachers. This can be overwhelming! Share these tips with students to help them be prepared for learning:

- **Plan locker visits.** "When do I need to go to my locker?"
- **Decide what you need for the next block of time.** "Do I have the books and materials I need until lunchtime?"

- **Take care of personal needs before going to class.** "Do I need to use the rest room?"
- **Review where instruction left off and anticipate where it is heading.** "What have we been studying and what happens next? What do I need to do to be ready?"
- **Review your notes and study guides.** "What did we do during class yesterday and how will that fit into what we do today?"
- **Determine the meaning of the lesson introduction.** "What should I learn today?"
- **Relax.** "What am I so worried about? I can keep up."

Try these tips to help students help themselves:

- Go over written directions with students who are having difficulty with their work. Help them find and highlight key words.
- Guide students in their independent reading. Instruct them to survey the material, read for key information, go back and study the key information until it is understood, then test themselves to see how well they know the material.

Rule of Thumb

A good rule of thumb: Teach your students how to link information they learn by connecting the first item with the second, and so on. This is an especially effective method for remembering steps in a problem or procedure.

Study Plan

Here is a study plan you can share with your students:

Planning

1. When your learning day is done, go straight to your study area and put your books and notebooks there.
2. Take out your notebook and look at your calendar and assignment book. See what you have to do to prepare for the next day. Also check the dates for upcoming tests and long-term assignments.
   - Keep in mind other commitments you have. (They should be on your calendar.)
   - Look at your assignments and estimate how long it will take you to finish each one.
   - Completing long-term projects and studying for tests require daily attention. Spend time on these tasks each day to be well-prepared.

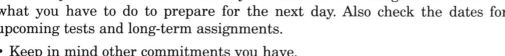

3. Get everything ready for the assignment you plan to do first. Put other books out of the way. It takes no more than five minutes to get ready for your study time. Do this every day—make it a habit.
4. Begin your first assignment at your regularly scheduled study time. Work through each assignment carefully and check off assignments in your notebook as you complete them.
   - If you have an assignment that expands on one you had the day before, briefly look back at the previous pages. That will help you focus on the subject.
5. Continue with all assignments and study as planned. Do your work thoroughly, and put your assignments in your notebook when you finish each one. Finally, check them off on your calendar.

NOTE-TAKING TIPS

Suggestions

Note-taking is one of the most frequently used strategies for learning material. Here are some tips that will help your students become better note-takers.

- Preview information before presenting it.
- Write key words, names, and definitions on a chart or chalkboard as you speak.
- When presenting lessons, make sure you are not talking too fast and that audiovisual materials are visible and audible to everyone.

- Teach your students to recognize note-taking cues. Point out that information written on the board or chart is one cue for note-taking. However, make sure your students know that the material written on the board is not the *only* information they need to record. Teach them to listen for certain verbal cue words or phrases. *Examples:* "First" or "The reason for" or "There are three causes." Other cues include repeated phrases or pauses by the speaker. Have your students brainstorm a list of other note-taking cues.

- Teach your students some "shorthand" methods for recording notes—symbols used in place of high-frequency words. These must be "read" later, so neatness counts!

- Provide skeletal notes—the basic content of what you plan to teach. Include headings, subheadings, key words or phrases, questions, etc. Leave blank spaces for your students to fill in remaining key information.

- Review your students' notes and suggest ways they can improve them. Periodically collect your students' notes. Your suggestions should be concrete and apply directly to the lesson's material.

- Let your students review each other's notes on the same material and describe their note-taking strategies to one another.

TEST-TAKING TRICKS

Teach your students to take control of their tests. Tell them to follow these test preparation steps:

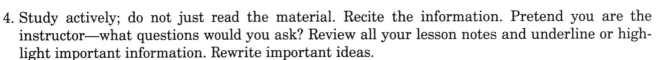

Steps to Take

1. Know exactly what material the test will cover. When a test is announced, write it on your calendar and in your assignment notebook.

2. Find out what type of test it will be, such as true/false or multiple choice, and study accordingly.

3. Plan when you will study for the test. Begin studying for it the day it is announced.

4. Study actively; do not just read the material. Recite the information. Pretend you are the instructor—what questions would you ask? Review all your lesson notes and underline or highlight important information. Rewrite important ideas.

5. Study with a buddy. Find a classmate who will be taking the test and review together.

6. Test yourself to determine how much you know and what you need to study.

7. Get a good night's sleep before your test.

Taking the Test

Communication

Points to remember when taking a test:

- Relax! If you have prepared for the test, you are ready.

- Look over the entire test before beginning to answer questions. Become familiar with the test. How long is it? What type of questions are on it?

- Answer the questions you know first. Put a mark by the ones you skip. Then go back and answer the questions you skipped. Be sure to answer all the questions.

- Check your test when you are finished. *Tip:* Avoid changing answers unless you are sure you made an error.

KEEPING IN TOUCH

As your students develop study habits, involve yourself in each step of the process. Remember, habits formed now will last throughout their lives! Confer with students often to assess their progress and management skills. This is especially vital in the early months of training.

Conferences with your students can be short—about five minutes is sufficient to touch base and assess progress. Ask questions that focus on their time management, organization, and study skills. Ask to see their calendars and assignment notebooks. Here are some suggested questions you may want to ask:

- How have you organized your learning time—at home and at school?
- What can you do to improve?
- What is your best study habit? Worst?
- Do you feel you are using your time efficiently?
- How do your study habits compare with your habits a week ago? A month ago?
- Are you having any particular trouble? How can I help?

Rule of Thumb

A good rule of thumb: Encourage your students to continually evaluate their work and study habits. By focusing on their strengths and weaknesses, they will become better organized and more productive.

SCHEDULE AND CHECKLIST

WEEKLY SCHEDULE

Name _____

Week of _____

Teacher _____

CODE: Art = A   Music = Mu.   Phys. Ed. = PE   Computer Lab = CL
Math = Ma.   Language Arts = LA   Reading = Rd.
Social Studies = SS   Science = S   Writing Workshop = WW
Health = H   Library/Media Center = LMC

YOUR CODES: _____ _____

_____ _____

Planning

TIME	MON.	TUES.	WED.	THURS.	FRI.	SAT.	SUN.

SPECIAL ACTIVITIES	TIME(S)	DAY(S)/DATES(S)	SPECIAL ACTIVITIES	TIME(S)	DAY(S)/DATE(S)

THINGS TO DO WEEK OF _____ ✔**when finished**

MON.	TUES.	WED.	THURS.	FRI.	SAT.	SUN.

Teaching Children Conflict Resolution

Do your students need encouragement to recognize their own feelings and the viewpoints of others, and to learn how to express and resolve their differences in productive ways? You can teach your students how to handle differences of opinion effectively. This chapter offers practical activities that will help you teach your students better communication, socialization, and problem-solving skills.

DIFFERENT OPINIONS

Getting into Focus

Sometimes it is a challenge for teachers to keep students from arguing or fighting. They often end up separating students who are having a disagreement.

The key is not to avoid conflict, but rather to teach students how to handle differences of opinion effectively. Students should be encouraged to discuss and explain their thoughts and feelings. When students can both verbalize their vantage points and listen to those of others, there is a greater chance that an agreement can be reached.

Ideas

Activity #1 Facts Versus Opinions

1. Present the following statements to your students:
- Tigers are a type of cat.
- Tigers have stripes.
- Tigers are prettier than lions.
- Tigers are endangered.
- Everyone should help protect endangered animals.

2. Review the difference between fact and opinion: A fact can be proved to be true. An opinion is a judgment, view, feeling, or belief. Ask students to identify each statement as fact or opinion.

3. Tell students that certain words signal that a statement is an opinion, for example, *prettier* and *should* in the sentences above. Have students identify the signal words in other sentences such as these:
- He's a great teacher. *(great)*
- I think it is too hot. *(think, too)*
- That was not fair! *(fair)*

4. Divide the class into small groups. Challenge each group to come up with a list of at least 20 words that signal judgment, comparison, viewpoint, or feeling.

5. Ask each group to read its list. Record all responses on a chart. (If a word is repeated, record it only once.) Save the chart for Activity #2.

Activity #2 Opinions Can Differ

1. Post the chart of opinion words from Activity #1. Use different words from the chart to write five opinion statements about subjects relevant to your students. List these on the chalkboard and underline the opinion words. *Example:* Math is <u>easier</u> than reading.

Communication

2. Direct each student to divide a sheet of paper into columns labeled *Statement, Agree, Disagree,* and *Don't Know.* Have the students copy the statements you wrote and check the columns that represent their opinions.

3. On the chalkboard, tally scores for each item and make a graph showing how many students responded in each of the columns.

4. Point out to the students that, unlike facts upon which everyone agrees, opinions can differ!

Statement	Agree	Disagree	Don't Know
1. Math is <u>easier</u> than reading.	✔		
2. Recycling is <u>too much</u> trouble.		✔	
3. Boys are <u>better</u> at sports than girls.	✔		
4. Having a computer is a <u>must</u>.			✔
5. Parents <u>should</u> monitor their children's television viewing.		✔	

Activity #3 Opinions Can Change

1. Ask each student to choose one of the five statements from Activity #2, take a position (agree or disagree), and write a persuasive essay to support that position. Remind students to use as many facts as possible to support their positions.

2. Let each student share his/her "argument" with the class, then repeat the opinion poll and tally as described in Activity #2.

3. Compare the graphs to see if and how the students' essays were able to sway the group's opinions.

Writing

Rule of Thumb

A good rule of thumb: It is important for students to realize that everyone has an opinion on an issue. They may agree with another person on some issues, yet disagree on others. Students must also realize that their opinions may change as they gain more information, or that they may influence the opinions of others.

WHAT IS CONFLICT?

Steps to Take

Conflict is a part of everyday life. A *conflict* occurs when people, ideas, or forces are in opposition. Teach students that conflict can produce positive or negative results.

1. Ask students to brainstorm synonyms for *conflict*. Record their responses on a chart. Circle all words that have a negative connotation, such as *fight*.

2. Ask students to describe examples of conflict in books or on television shows and how the conflicts were resolved. Ask the students to speculate about what a story would be like without conflict.

3. Introduce the concept of conflict as potentially being good. Tell students that conflict sometimes leads to a better idea or solution to a problem. *Example:* A disagreement about which of two movies to watch leads a family to watch a third one, which they all enjoy. Have students state ways that conflict can produce positive results.

4. Explain to students that conflict can occur between people with differing opinions, or within ourselves when we have mixed feelings. Conflict can be positive when we learn from it or negative if we allow it to cause greater difficulties. Oftentimes how we choose to resolve conflict determines the outcome.

COMPETITION VERSUS COLLABORATION

Getting into Focus

When resolving conflicts, one person does not have to lose in order for the other person to win. A collaborative approach, rather than a competitive one, is more beneficial to both people.

Unlike competitive sports, interpersonal interactions do not require that there be a loser. Many conflicts can be resolved so that both parties are winners. The following example demonstrates for students the potential outcomes when two people have independent goals.

Juan and Dario are cousins who have not seen each other for many months, so they wish to spend as much time together as possible for the next two days. Juan wants to go to the beach and Dario wants to play football. There are four possible solutions:

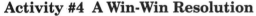

> *Win-Lose Situation*
> They both go to the beach.
>
> *Lose-Win Situation*
> They both go to the park and play football.
>
> *Lose-Lose Situation*
> They spend all their time arguing and neither one goes to the beach or plays football.
>
> *Win-Win Situation*
> They play football at the beach.

Have students come up with other conflictual situations and the four possible solutions: Win-Lose, Lose-Win, Lose-Lose, and Win-Win.

Activity #4 A Win-Win Resolution
Let students practice resolving a conflict through cooperation. Present the following conflictual situation: *Sara is getting ready to start her work when she discovers that her pencil is gone. She notices that Mary has a pencil that looks just like the one she is missing. Sara accuses Mary of taking her pencil. Mary denies it.*

Ideas

Have students pair up. Challenge them to come up with a solution to the conflict so that each person wins and neither is left feeling cheated, hurt, or unfairly treated.

After allowing students a few minutes to discuss the problem and the possible solutions, ask pairs to share their results with the rest of the group—not just their recommended resolution, but also the process they used to arrive at it.

COMMUNICATION

Getting into Focus

There are many aspects to communication. Explore with your students the complexity of verbal, written, and nonverbal communication.

Verbal and Written Communication

Activities #5, #6, and #7 illustrate how communication can go astray, from the perspective of both the sender and the receiver of the message.

Activity #5 What Did You Say?

Here is a quick way of demonstrating to students that an oral message can become jumbled beyond recognition:

Instruct students to sit in a circle, shoulder to shoulder. Inform them that you will whisper an important message to the first student, who must whisper it to the second student, and so on, until the message is conveyed all the way around the circle and the last student whispers it to you. At that point, share verbatim the final message you received and compare it to the initial message.

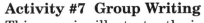

. . . Make waves across the center of the page. Draw a sun in the corner. . . .

Activity #6 Giving and Receiving Directions

This revealing activity shows just how important details are in giving and receiving directions. The object is to produce two identical drawings without any visual clues.

1. Have pairs of students sit back to back, each with a pad of paper and a pencil. Have one person begin drawing a picture. As he draws, he is to give step-by-step directions to his partner for drawing the same thing.

2. Directions are to be given orally. Neither person can look at the other's drawing until it is finished. The person giving directions should be as precise as possible.

3. Ask students to compare their finished drawings. (They are likely to be quite different!) Have each pair discuss how the directions could have been better. *Example:* "You said to draw a sun in the corner. You should have said in which corner and how big to make it."

4. Have students switch roles and try again.

Activity #7 Group Writing

This exercise illustrates the importance of *continuity in communication*. It is not just the last message that is important but the whole context of the conversation.

Writing

Have students count off from 1 to 6 to form groups of six. Student 1 writes the first line of a story. Student 2 reads the first sentence, adds a second sentence, then folds the paper over so that only the second sentence is visible. Student 3 writes a third sentence (seeing only the second), and folds the paper over so that only the third sentence is visible. Continue until everyone has written three sentences, then read the stories aloud.

I Messages

Communication

An *"I message"* is one that states a feeling—"I feel sad when you . . ." A *"you message"* is one that places blame or criticizes—"You never . . ."

Teach your students that *you messages* make the other person feel attacked and therefore defensive. This often escalates a conflict. *I messages* allow a person to express feelings and needs without attacking. When both parties use *I messages,* their needs are clearly expressed and they can cooperate to solve their conflict.

To give a clear *I message* say:

1. **I feel . . . (state your feeling).** State a specific feeling (sad, mad, happy, scared) rather than a thought ("that you were mean").

2. **When you . . . (state the behavior of the other person).** State what occurred ("borrowed my baseball glove without asking me"), not your interpretation of the action or behavior.

3. **Because . . . (state the effect of that behavior upon you).** Be specific. ("I did not have my glove when the baseball game started.")

As with any new material, students need to practice, practice, practice. Here are some suggestions:

Suggestions

1. Present scenarios, such as the ones below, and have students complete this statement: "I feel . . . when you/I . . . because . . ." Use both positive and negative situations.

   - *Your best friend says she is moving to another state.*
   - *Someone calls you a name.*
   - *Your team wins the big game.*
   - *Your uncle forgets your birthday.*
   - *Your mom assumes you didn't clean your room.*
   - *Someone hits you because you are short.*
   - *You spent your allowance on a special gift for someone.*

2. Give each student a list of eight conflictual situations. *Example:* You are working at the computer with a partner. Suddenly you hear a POP and the screen goes blank. Your partner says, "I'm telling. You broke the computer."

   Have students write three *I message* statements for each scenario. Review these as a group. Record responses on the chalkboard.

3. Pair students for role-playing. Give each pair a card describing a conflict. Have them alternate being an angry person and a person who is actively practicing the I message technique.

4. Challenge students to rewrite *you messages* as *I messages.* Use these or other relevant examples:

   - *You always pick her before me.*
   - *You never paid me back for the money I gave you.*
   - *Do you always have to be first in line?*
   - *You're the one who made us late for school.*
   - *You always win. You probably cheat.*
   - *You think you're better than me.*
   - *You didn't call me back last night.*
   - *Why do you think you can change the channel while I am watching something?*

5. Encourage students to use *I messages* at home.

Communication

Nonverbal Communication

Nonverbal messages can be stumbling blocks to conflict resolution. Most students are not aware that they convey messages by body posture, facial expression, and eye contact. Use these activities to increase their awareness of body language.

Activity #8 Awareness of Nonverbal Messages

Set up small groups to play "feelings charades." The performer is not allowed to talk but must use body posture and facial expressions to convey a mood to team members. Make sets of cards listing eight common feelings, such as *scared, excited, worried, surprised, tired, confused, angry,* and *pleased.* Give each team the same cards in a different order. Then see which team guesses the eight feelings in the shortest time. Discuss which nonverbal gestures/characteristics were most effective in depicting particular moods.

Getting into Focus

LISTENING

Listening may seem like a passive activity, but effective listening demands action on the part of the listener! Communication is a two-way street that requires response to the other person as well as self-expression. Active listening, therefore, requires considerable energy and concentrated attention. The payoff is better communication between people.

Active Listening Goals

An active listener should keep these goals in mind:

- To understand thoroughly what the speaker is communicating.
- To assure the speaker that you understand.

Activity #9 Active Listening

1. Review "Awareness of Nonverbal Messages."

2. Ask for a student volunteer to talk while you demonstrate the use of these *nonverbal* signs of listening:

  - making eye contact
  - facing the speaker
  - squaring shoulders toward the speaker
  - sitting/standing up straight
  - keeping hands and feet still
  - having an open posture (arms and legs uncrossed)
  - leaning forward a little
  - appearing interested
  - maintaining a smile or a positive expression
  - nodding your head

3. Demonstrate these *verbal* signs of listening:

   • saying "yes" or "uh-huh"

   • paraphrasing the speaker's statements

   • summarizing the speaker's statements

   • asking related questions

   • encouraging the other person to continue talking

4. Ask two student volunteers to come forward. Direct one child to talk and the other to demonstrate good active listening skills. Have each student in the audience write down signs of good listening skills that they observe. Discuss the aspects of active listening that were noted in the demonstration.

Listening for Feelings

Getting into Focus

Not only is it important to listen to the content of what another is saying, it is equally important to listen to the feelings being conveyed. Point out to your students these aspects of listening for feelings:

• Everybody has feelings.

• There is not a right or wrong way to feel in a situation; everyone has a unique reaction.

• Letting people know how you feel helps them to understand your situation and behavior.

• Many times we have to figure out or ask others how they are feeling because they do not directly tell us.

Ideas

Activity #10 Can You Hear Feelings?

1. Invite a student volunteer to describe something that happened to him or her last weekend. Ask student listeners to describe the feelings of the speaker, as well as the nonverbal indicators that pointed to them. Verify students' impressions with the speaker.

2. Divide your students into pairs. Ask them to alternate speaking on different topics. Tell the listeners to follow these steps:

   • Use good active listening techniques.

   • Identify the speaker's feelings.

   • Indicate what led to their impressions.

   • Request confirmation from the speaker.

RESOLVING CONFLICTS

Help students see that there may be more than one solution to a problem or conflict. Explore different approaches to resolving conflicts, such as brainstorming, problem-solving steps, and role-playing. Encourage students to be aware of others' feelings and to consider the consequences of various actions.

Brainstorming

Brainstorming is a technique used to generate a long list of diverse responses without making judgments about individual ideas.

Steps to Take

Activity #11 Brainstorming

1. Explain the objective of brainstorming (above).

2. Establish a short time limit (2 minutes).

3. Tell students to proceed as follows:
   - Call out their immediate responses.
   - Say anything that comes to mind.
   - Generate as many responses as possible.
   - Avoid judging the quality of responses.
   - Be creative—the more extraordinary the better.

4. Remind students that there are no correct or incorrect responses.

5. Announce the topic.

6. Record all responses on the chalkboard.

7. When the time is up, stop!

Rule of Thumb

A good rule of thumb: Brainstorming is a technique used in many different situations that call for a "storm" of ideas. It is important that students learn how to generate ideas without prejudgment. The object is to go back later and eliminate ideas that are not feasible. Anytime you use brainstorming, remind students to go for quantity, creativity, and ingenuity.

Problem-Solving Steps

Teach students to follow these steps when faced with a person-to-person conflict:

1. Identify the problem.

2. Determine what each person wants and feels.

3. Brainstorm ways to solve the problem.

4. Determine the consequences of each solution.

5. Choose what you believe to be the best solution.

6. Evaluate whether your chosen solution solves the problem.

7. If the problem is not solved, return to the step that needs clarification or more input.

8. Continue the process until you are satisfied with the solution.

Steps to Take

Ideas

Activity #12 Can You Act Out a Solution?
Give students practice using the problem-solving steps from the previous page. Write out the beginning of a story that sets up a conflict, such as the example below. Give pairs of students a copy of the storystarter and ask them to use the problem-solving steps to arrive at a possible solution. Ask the pair to write an ending to the story that includes their solution. Have several pairs of students act out the story to the conclusion. Then let the group evaluate the different solutions presented.

It is Saturday afternoon. Joe and his best friend, Ricky, are in Joe's room. Ricky picks up a ball and starts tossing it in the air. Joe says, "Hey, don't do that! You could break something and I'll get in trouble." Ricky says, "You don't trust me?" and he tosses the ball even higher. Joe says, "Stop it!" and goes for the ball as it is coming down. Ricky goes for it, too. The boys collide and the ball knocks over a lamp. "Now look what you've done!" shout both boys at once. . . .

Rule of Thumb

A good rule of thumb: It is best to use hypothetical examples of conflicts to practice problem solving, not students' real-life conflicts or problems. Never require students to participate in situations that expose personal information or problems, even anonymously!

RESPONSES TO CONFLICT

There are a variety of ways people respond to conflict. Help students see that different responses are called for under different conditions. Explain the following three types of responses and the circumstances under which each is most appropriate:

- *Work together*—This response works well to solve most disagreements between people. *Example:* A group project is assigned and the members disagree on how to do it.

- *Walk away or comply*—This response is appropriate when the conflict presents an immediate danger. *Example:* Someone threatens to harm you. *Note:* In most cases, you will want enlist the help of an outside authority after the danger has passed.

- *Act immediately*—This response is needed when you must act quickly to prevent an accident or disaster. *Example:* Even though you are not supposed to use the phone, you smell smoke and call 911.

Rule of Thumb

A good rule of thumb: Use your judgment to determine how deeply to get into conflict issues with your students. Let their ages and maturity levels guide you. For example, young students tend to think in "black and white"; there is a right or wrong answer, and it is more than likely that they will simply want you to decide. Older students, however, are not only faced with conflicts among themselves, but they are also often dealing with internal conflicts that they may not understand. More mature students need to know that not all conflicts can be solved, but that it is well worth trying. Like the ostrich analogy, ignoring the problem does not make it go away.

STUDENTS SOLVING THEIR OWN CONFLICTS

Students can be taught to solve many of their own conflicts without the assistance of an adult. When two students are faced with a real-life conflict, suggest that they take these steps to successful conflict management:

Suggestions

1. Decide if you want to resolve the conflict yourselves. Talk and agree that you will work on the problem together.

2. Each of you, in turn, explains the conflict from your vantage point. The speaker uses *I messages* and the listener uses active-listening techniques.

3. Each participant verbally verifies and summarizes the other person's feelings.

4. Both of you write down your own and the other person's positions, interests, and underlying needs.

5. Brainstorm together as many solutions to the conflict as possible.

6. Discuss the positive and negative consequences of each solution and mutually agree upon the one you think could work best.

7. Try the chosen solution.

8. Through verbal discussion, evaluate whether the chosen solution is working.

9. If the solution is working, reinforce each other's efforts and follow through. If the solution is not working, go back as far as necessary to rework the problem and proceed until you are successful.

Rule of Thumb

A good rule of thumb: Impress upon students that it is best to use these techniques of conflict resolution when each participant is in a calm and rational state of mind. Remind them that attempts to solve issues or to communicate effectively are generally unsuccessful if they are extremely angry or emotional. Suggest that they walk away until the "flash" has passed.

Building Self-Esteem

Provide a learning environment that recognizes and celebrates each of your students' contributions to your class! High self-esteem is one of the most valuable assets a person can possess. Having high self-esteem fosters a healthy sense of self and a positive outlook on life. This chapter will help you better understand the nature of self-esteem and how it develops, and the information and activities suggest ways in which you can foster high self-esteem in your students.

WHAT IS SELF-ESTEEM?

Getting into Focus

Webster defines self-esteem as "a confidence and satisfaction in oneself." Put another way, self-esteem is self-approval, or a sense that one is lovable and capable. People who have high self-esteem are confident, resourceful, independent, and responsible. They accept challenges with enthusiasm and are willing to take risks in order to reach their full potential.

People with low self-esteem, on the other hand, lack confidence in themselves and need constant reassurance. They are overly sensitive and often withdrawn. They become easily frustrated when confronted with problems or upsets. In short, people with low self-esteem avoid taking challenges such as trying new activities or acquiring new skills, and they have difficulty handling competition, rejection, and failure.

It is easy to see that a person's well-being depends greatly on how he sees and values himself. High self-esteem, or a "positive self-image" is crucial to one's ability to form satisfying relationships with other people, to deal effectively with life's stresses, and to make meaningful contributions to society. Building children's self-esteem and giving them healthy views of themselves are goals that parents and teachers need to work toward in order to help children discover their full potential and become happy, successful adults.

CHILDREN AND SELF-ESTEEM

For children, self-esteem develops mainly through their relationships with other people. This is because children do not have the ability to learn about themselves directly. Instead, they see themselves through their interactions with the people who are close to them. For very young children, self-esteem develops primarily through their relationships with their parents. A child who is loved and valued sees herself as being lovable and important; a child who is neglected or rejected feels she is unlovable and worthless.

As children grow older, teachers and friends become influential factors in their lives. Just as positive experiences in the home form the foundation for self-esteem, positive experiences at school contribute to the development of children's awareness and acceptance of themselves.

SELF-ESTEEM IN THE CLASSROOM

Rule of Thumb

It is important to realize that children do not gain self-esteem by instruction. In fact, no program in itself will make children like or value themselves. As has already been mentioned, relationships and interaction with people form the foundation for children's self-esteem. As children are loved and respected, they come to see themselves as being worthy of love and respect. At school, this same principle applies. The teacher may initiate activities to encourage self-esteem, but in the long run, it is the quality of the teacher-student relationship and the meaningful, personal interactions that take place within school that most influence how children feel about themselves. In other words, children gain self-esteem when they are treated with esteem. The following pages present suggestions and strategies for applying this "rule of thumb" in the classroom.

FOUR FACTORS FOR SELF-ESTEEM

Getting into Focus

Stephanie Marston, in her book *The Magic of Encouragement* (William Morrow and Company, 1990), points out four factors that she believes are critical to the development of high self-esteem: *belonging, uniqueness, power,* and *self-expression*.

Each of these factors defines a particular type of basic emotional need. Every child has a need to "fit in" with his family and with society as a whole. Every child has a need to feel she is an individual and that she has qualities that are special and unique. Every child needs to feel he is in control of certain aspects of his life and that he has some influence on what goes on around him. And finally, every child needs to feel she can honestly express her thoughts and feelings and that she has the freedom to ask questions.

When a child's basic emotional needs are satisfied, his self-esteem grows and develops. In the following sections, the four factors for self-esteem are discussed within the context of the school environment.

A SENSE OF BELONGING

Getting into Focus

Children, like adults, need to feel emotionally connected to the people who are important to them. These connections give them a sense of belonging that results in feelings of security and contentedness. At first, this sense of belonging is established through relationships with family members. As children experience love, they feel special and important, and they come to see themselves as a vital part of their family groups. Later, as outside groups such as school and clubs enter children's lives, teachers play key roles in helping students develop a sense of belonging.

Helping Children Feel They Belong

Suggestions

It is essential for students to feel welcome and relaxed in the classroom and for them to understand that their contributions to the class are important. Here are some suggestions for helping students feel they are valued members of the class.

Respect

Let the students know they are important.

• Be available to students, whether they want to ask you school-related questions or they simply want to share something with you. Greeting students as they arrive through the door or staying after school just to let them talk with you communicates the fact that you value being with the class.

• Get to know each student. Listen to what students are saying, even in casual conversation, and tune in to the things a student is interested in or curious about. If a student communicates that he is interested in dinosaurs, bring a dinosaur book to class for him to read. When students see that their interests and concerns are important to you, they feel important.

• Share your own personal information with the class. Let students know about your family, hobbies, interests, and goals. As you and the class get to know one another, bonds of mutual trust and respect are established.

• Express appreciation when students are especially helpful and cooperative. Letting students know that they have an impact on how you feel confirms to them that they are valued human beings.

Encourage cooperation and teamwork.

• Give the class opportunities to work in pairs or small groups. Vary the groups during the year so that students have a chance to work with different partners. As students work together and learn from one another, they see that individual contributions count.

Participation

• Let groups share their work with the class. Then have students comment on what they liked about each activity or what they learned from the different presentations. Having the class respond to their work gives students important feedback about what they did.

• Make sure you ask every student to take on classroom responsibilities such as handing out papers or cleaning the chalkboard. These responsibilities let children know they are needed to help the class in particular ways.

- Provide opportunities for the whole class to work toward one goal, such as tidying up the classroom, decorating the hallway, or putting on a play. A class effort results in an accomplishment in which everyone can take pride.

- Set up a buddy system with an older or younger class, and let students write letters to one another or read together. Older students can tutor younger ones in reading, math, or other subject areas; younger children can draw pictures or write stories for their partners. During the year, let your students show their appreciation to the other class by having them write thank-you notes or design "appreciation awards" for their buddies.

Capture group memories.
- Take photos of your class working together and post the pictures on a bulletin board or place them in a photo album. Seeing these pictures can strengthen the feeling of connection students have with one another.

- Every few months, have each student contribute one page to a "Classroom Book of Memories." The pages in the book should describe school events or activities that students have especially enjoyed. As students read these pages, they will be reminded about the good times they have shared.

A SENSE OF UNIQUENESS

Getting into Focus

No two people are exactly alike. Every person's individual makeup is influenced by such factors as cultural background, family upbringing, inborn talents, and personal preferences. At school, teachers can enhance creativity and learning by recognizing each student's uniqueness and building on her particular strengths. When children know they are appreciated as individuals, they learn to accept and respect themselves, and in turn, they are able to see and appreciate the uniqueness of others.

Helping Children Feel Unique and Special

Involving students in activities that focus on the self is a common practice among teachers. Many classrooms, for example, display booklets or bulletin boards titled *"All About Me"* or *"I Am Special Because . . ."* While these activities might raise students' consciousness of who they are, teachers can better develop self-esteem by encouraging each student to examine how his special qualities enable him to be a unique and important member of his family, his class, and the world at large. The following ideas will help you create a learning environment that celebrates uniqueness and guides students into seeing themselves as participants in the world around them.

Suggestions

Participation

Let students explore and appreciate differences.
• Discuss with the class the fact that people have different interests, talents, and abilities, and that everyone has something she can do well. Let children know that one person might be skilled in math, another good in baseball, and another knowledgeable about pets. Emphasize that regardless of people's abilities, what is important is that a person tries her best in whatever she undertakes.

• Give students opportunities to teach one another. For example, a student who is a good reader can listen to and encourage a student who is not; a student who knows a game can teach a group how to play; a student can share with the class about a family or cultural tradition.

• Share your own personal strengths. Tell the class which of your qualities have helped you in your teaching. Then let each student talk about his strengths and share the type of work he might enjoy when he grows up.

Awareness

Build on individual strengths and interests.
• Respect students' individual abilities and strengths, and be sensitive to the fact that students learn at different speeds and achieve varying levels of mastery. Reward the effort each child makes and help her recognize the progress she has made.

• Create an environment where students feel free to investigate, explore, and create on their own. Display how-to books on crafts, games, science experiments, magic tricks, and other activities, and encourage students to try the ideas in their spare time. Or, let students pursue constructive activities of their choice (such as writing, listening to a taped story, reading, drawing, or building). Afterward, have the students share their investigations, discoveries, and creations with the class.

- During the school week, take time to let each student know you have noticed her in class. For example, you might praise a student who is working hard learning a new skill or voice appreciation to a student who has helped a fellow classmate. Recognizing individual accomplishments reinforces to students that you see each of them as a unique, special human being.

A SENSE OF POWER

Getting into Focus

Both children and adults need to feel they have some control over their lives and that they are in charge of certain aspects of their environments. In general, this fundamental need is fulfilled when a person is given opportunities to make decisions, set goals, and solve problems. These experiences help develop a sense of independence and personal power which, in turn, results in feelings of confidence and competence.

Helping Students Gain a Sense of Power

Students gain a sense of personal power when they see themselves as decision makers, goal setters, and problem solvers. When students feel competent in these three roles, their self-esteems are heightened greatly. Here are some suggestions for helping students realize that they have the power to positively influence their circumstances and make a difference in what goes on around them.

Suggestions

Awareness

Involve students in decision making.

Allowing students to make decisions about things that really matter to them lets them know that you trust their abilities to make choices. Letting students make decisions helps them feel responsible and important. Opportunities for decision making can include the following:

- Classroom Rules—Together with your students decide on what rules should be followed in order to make the classroom a pleasant, productive learning environment.

- Activities—Give students a certain amount of control over classroom activities. For example, let students suggest topics for discussion or research, select activities to do during their spare time, or choose the types of displays to make for an Open House and other special events.

- Solutions to Problems—Guide students into making thoughtful, realistic decisions about problems. For example, students can discuss ways they can help a classmate who has a lengthy illness or two children who have a difficult time working together can be given the responsibility of choosing what to do to make the situation better.

Participation

Encourage students to meet challenges and work toward their goals.

- Discuss the fact that success at school comes from making an effort to try new skills or tasks and by actively participating in what goes on in the classroom. Let students know that each of them can make a difference in his or her capacity to learn and grow.

- Remind students that they are "competing" against themselves, not their classmates. Help students keep track of their individual progress by providing each child with a folder for keeping samples of work. Every few weeks, let each student examine her folder and compare past performance with her current work. Students will be amazed and pleased at how much they have accomplished!

- Motivate students by showing you are genuinely interested in your class. Teachers, of course, are in school to facilitate learning and to help students meet certain criteria for academic success. But when you take time to talk to each student about his goals, ask questions about his interests, or listen to his concerns, you let him know that the two of you are partners in his learning.

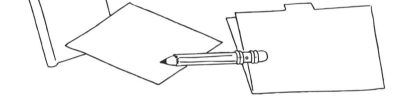

- Give opportunities for students to achieve success in small steps. For example, a student who is having difficulty mastering addition facts can target two facts to learn every week; a child who wants to be able to run one mile (1.6 km) a day can start out by running a shorter distance.

- Praise students for their efforts and build on each student's successes. As students reach their goals, their self-confidences increase and they are able to meet new challenges with eagerness and enthusiasm.

Encourage students to solve problems and learn from setbacks.
Problems are a part of life. Yet, however unpleasant, they are critical to children's development. When children learn how to deal constructively with upsets and make a real effort to overcome obstacles, they gain a sense of mastery over their environments, and their self-esteem grows. Teachers can nurture self-esteem by helping students become confident problem-solvers.

Awareness

- Help students see that setbacks are temporary. Sometimes, simply talking about the problem helps a student see the situation in a more positive light.

- Listen to students' concerns and acknowledge their feelings of sadness, disappointment, frustration, or anger. At the same time, indicate to them that they have the choice of trying again. For example, a student who does not solve a math question the first time can, with or without your help, go through the problem-solving process once more; a student who has trouble completing a creative writing assignment can put away the task for awhile and then try writing later.

- Help students see failures as part of the learning process. Point out that through failures people learn what does not work, and this discovery often leads to new ideas or new solutions. (Thomas Edison had to try 10,000 times before he made a workable electric lightbulb!)

- Be supportive and encouraging by sharing your own childhood disappointments, failures, and successes. As parents, teachers, and other adults model how to handle problems and setbacks, students gain confidence in their own abilities to deal with life's challenges.

FREEDOM OF EXPRESSION

Getting into Focus

Every person has a need to feel that she is accepted for who she is and that her thoughts, feelings, and personal convictions count. When people are allowed to express themselves openly and honestly, there is opportunity for the development of meaningful communication and mutual respect. For children, the need to express their own thoughts and feelings is especially important because it allows them to grow into individuals who have a strong sense of who they are. Knowing that their ideas are heard and their feelings accepted give children a sense of importance and self-worth.

Suggestions

Allowing Children Freedom of Expression

Children need to be allowed to express themselves and to ask questions in order to gain a sense of their individuality and inner self. Here are some ideas for creating a learning environment that encourages self-expression and acceptance among students.

Take students' thoughts and feelings seriously.

- Listen to what students say and respond to their words with respect. When students feel you sincerely care about what they think and feel, they are more willing to voice their true thoughts and feelings.

- Discuss with students the fact that everyone has his own ideas and opinions. Explain that though points of view differ, each person's thoughts need to be respected.

Respect

- Help students understand that along with freedom of expression comes the responsibility to be considerate. Ask students to suggest times when it is better to be silent because feelings may get hurt (for example, when a person's appearance is criticized) or because the timing is inappropriate (it is not their turn to speak).

• Ask students to share how they feel about school events, a newspaper story, and other issues. Share your responses as well. Students who are allowed to honestly express their thoughts and feelings grow into adults who are able to form loving relationships based on openness and trust.

Let students know they can ask questions.
It is essential for students to feel they can ask questions without fear of being ridiculed or reprimanded. At the same time, students must learn that they will not always get satisfactory answers to their questions or receive everything they ask for. At school, students need to know they can:

• ask questions about things they do not understand or things that make them curious,

• ask for help,

• express their needs and wants,

• make suggestions for improvements, and

• express positive and negative feelings, as long as it is done with respect.

Allowing students to ask questions fosters independence and high self-esteem, and gives students increased ability to accept and respect other people's thoughts and feelings.

DISCIPLINE AND SELF-ESTEEM

Getting into Focus

Self-esteem grows and develops when children feel secure and safe in their environments. This sense of security and safety is nurtured when adults set firm, clear limits and guidelines.

Discipline in the classroom is an important factor in the teacher-student relationship. Students feel secure when they know what the rules for behavior are and what you expect of them. It is crucial that discipline be applied consistently in order to be effective. When students know you mean what you say, they are able to place their trust in you.

The purpose of discipline is not to punish nor is it to damage children's feelings of self-worth. On the contrary, effective discipline keeps self-esteem intact and helps children grow into confident, responsible adults. Here are some pointers for establishing and maintaining effective discipline in your classroom:

• Stress cooperation. Let students know that what they do has an impact on the whole class.

• See your students as responsible individuals. Students respond to the expectations parents and teachers have of them. When expectations are positive, they behave in positive ways.

• Teach students that their behavior is based on personal choice and that this freedom of choice is coupled with responsibility. As students learn to take responsibility for their actions, they develop the self-discipline needed to make wise choices in the future.

• Use consequences that are reasonable and that make sense. For example, if a student bothers a classmate at recess, making him sit by himself until he can play cooperatively is a more reasonable consequence than keeping him after school for detention.

BUILDING SELF-ESTEEM:
AN ONGOING COMMITMENT

Getting into Focus

Building children's self-esteem is an ongoing commitment that needs the involvement and support of both parents and teachers. It is important to keep the lines of communication open between home and school in order to ensure that the specific needs and circumstances of each child are addressed.

Statistics show that, in general, younger students have a more positive view of themselves than do older ones. Perhaps one reason lies in the fact that as children get older, the criteria for self-esteem change. In the very early years of life, children are accepted and valued simply for having been born. Later, as they begin to participate in the world around them, certain standards and expectations are imposed. As the years go by, a child's self-esteem may suffer numerous blows due to criticisms, scoldings, comparisons with others, rejections, and failures. By the time many children reach adolescence, their feelings of self-worth may have greatly diminished.

Teachers can make a difference, though, in how children see themselves and can help students acquire the skills to handle life's stresses. As teachers and students work together in an environment that fosters respect, cooperation, and acceptance, children learn that ultimately they have the power to control their own lives.

Improving Writing Skills

Give your students a powerful tool of communication—their own words! This chapter will help you incorporate writing across the curriculum, confer with young writers, motivate your writers to revise and correct their work, and help them plan, focus on, and organize their writing. You will also find specific writing activities and concrete ways to effectively monitor and evaluate your students' progress.

PREPARING POWER WRITERS

Suggestions

Prepare your students to be "power writers" through a writing program that incorporates these components:

- **Writing Time**—Provide your students with regular time slots to think, write, confer, read, rework ideas, and rewrite. Writers need time to spend on their work.

- **Topics**—Encourage your students to use writing as a way to express their ideas, interests, thoughts, and concerns. Students write best about topics that matter to them and for audiences who are interested in their ideas.

- **Feedback**—Allow time and opportunities for students to get feedback on their writing while their work is in progress. Constructive comments from you and from their peers provide helpful feedback.

- **Mechanics Instruction**—Address errors as they occur in your student's writing. The mechanics of writing, including spelling strategies and grammar rules, are more meaningful if taught "on the spot."

- **Models**—Expose your students to your own writing and that of authors, peers, and adults. Models can be written products or the writers themselves.

- **Reading Time**—Provide your students with a wide variety of reading materials on which to reflect.

- **Cross-Curriculum Integration**—Let students write in all subject areas. Writing gives students a means to move from observation to reaction and reflection—a powerful tool for learning in any content area.

- **Guidance**—Be enthusiastic, well prepared, and organized when teaching writing.

Rule of Thumb

A good rule of thumb: When students are taught to respond to others' work thoughtfully, they can effectively critique and teach each other.

THE WRITING PROCESS

By teaching writing as a process rather than a product, you equip your students with a terrific tool—their own words—to use at their command. Teaching writing as a process enables your students to *use* writing rather than just produce it. A process approach to writing instruction involves five stages:

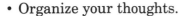
Steps to Take

1. **Prewriting**—Activities to generate ideas for writing. Motivate students to write by means of discussions, questions, games, illustrations, brainstorming activities, etc. At this stage of the writing process, ask your students to take these steps:

   • Think about who will read your writing and why.

   • Form ideas, gather information, brainstorm, read, and observe.

   • Think about what you want to say and how you want to say it.

2. **Drafting**—The first writing. As they begin to write, tell your students to keep in mind their audiences and their purposes for writing. They should also consider the form in which their work will be published. At this stage, allow your writers to focus on expressing thoughts and feelings—do not worry about the mechanics of the writing. Offer your writers support and encouragement, answer questions, and confer with them. During the drafting stage of the writing process, instruct your students to take these steps:

• Organize your thoughts.

• Choose ideas and develop them.

• Sequence your ideas.

• Write your first draft.

• Get feedback from others.

Steps to Take

3. **Revising**—Reevaluation and editing for content and style. Teach your students to consider the suggestions of their peers, rearrange ideas, and make changes to make their writing more clear. Give them time to rethink how to communicate their ideas more effectively. During the revising state of the writing process, tell your writers to take these steps:

   • Reread what you wrote.

   • Consider what others say about your work.

   • Add or delete parts, select better words or ideas, rearrange ideas, replace any unclear ideas, and complete any ideas that are not finished.

4. **Proofreading**—Checking grammar, spelling, mechanics, and neatness. Guide your students to find as many errors as they can on their own, then have them pass their work on to peers for rechecking. Your writers can then correct errors as they prepare final drafts. During this stage of the writing process instruct your students to take these steps:

• Make sure all sentences are complete.

• Check spelling, capitalization, and punctuation.

• Look for words used incorrectly.

• Have a partner recheck your work.

• Recopy the work neatly and correctly.

5. **Publishing**—Sharing writing with an audience. Publishing the writing may take any number of forms, such as displaying it, reading it aloud, binding it into a book, recording it on tape, performing it, illustrating it, setting it to music, or talking about it with others.

A good rule of thumb: Tell your students that not all of their writing needs to be shared. Sometimes, they will want to write just for themselves. This personal expression can and should remain private!

Rule of Thumb

"WRITER'S BLOCK" BREAKERS

Use motivating prewriting activities, such as games, puzzles, and challenges, to get writing flowing.

• **Automatic Writing**—Get the words flowing! Set a timer. Tell your students to write whatever comes into their minds. It does not have to make sense or even be in complete sentences. If they keep having the same thoughts, they should write them over and over again. If they get distracted by something, they should write about that. If they are "stuck," they can write down the names of things around them. The key is to keep writing!

• **Sassy Sentences**—Use alliteration as motivation! Create a sentence in which each word begins with the same letter. *Example:* "Amy Arnold's aunt ate an angry ant." Instruct your students to write the same kind of sentences for as many letters of the alphabet as they can.

• **Mind Message**—Association gets writing going! Ask students to write a word and then list other words, ideas, or places it brings to mind—anything they think of that relates to the word. *Example:* Football—game, noise, win, excitement, team, hot dog. Now, ask the students to look through the words they have listed for story ideas. Challenge them to write a title and a story or paragraph based on words from their lists.

• **How To**—Use simple know-how! Ask each student to write out the specific steps involved in performing a task, such as brushing teeth, tying a shoelace, turning on a computer, or making a bed. Tell students to use detailed but easy-to-understand directions and to be careful not to leave out any part of the process.

• **Super Similies**—Similies make writing as easy as pie! Introduce similies to your students. A simile is a comparison using like or as. Give several examples, then ask the students to write or complete similies. *Examples: yellow like a . . . , creaked like a . . . , laughed like . . . , as red as . . . , as bright as . . . , as dry as . . . , as loud as . . . , as smart as . . .*

FOCUSING IN

Once prewriting activities have produced ideas for writing, the next step is to write a draft. Suggest that students begin with a topic passage, or lead—one to three sentences that define the topic or lead the reader into the work. How the lead or topic passage is crafted depends on the type of work. The first few lines of a report on insects would be quite different from those of a mystery story! Here are some tips for helping your students focus on using leads and topic passages.

Suggestions

• Keep the lead short. Even a long written work can flow from a few carefully crafted sentences.

- In story leads, include elements that create a sense of anticipation. *Example:* "The day began much like any other. Then there was a knock at the door. I wasn't expecting anyone."

- Spend the time you need to write the lead or topic passage. Rewrite it several times if necessary until it says exactly what you want and guides you effectively in writing the rest of the work.

- If, after several tries, you have trouble narrowing your topic or writing your lead, try writing part of your passage. See where your writing is headed, then go back and try the topic passage again.

- Write a topic passage that eases the reader into the written work. A question is sometimes effective in getting the reader to want to read further. *Example:* "Did you know that there is an animal that is both male and female?"

- Include interesting or important words at the beginning and end of your topic introduction. *Example:* "Saturday, August 26, was a hot and sticky night, but not too hot for a robbery."

Rule of Thumb

A good rule of thumb: Let students know that fresh ideas sometimes surface during writing. The writer then has to decide if she should stick to the original plan or rewrite the lead to incorporate the new ideas.

WRITING CONFERENCES

Communication

The writing conference is an integral aspect of "growing" good writers. The following techniques will help you keep your young writers on track:

- **Assigned Conferences**—Set up a specific time to meet with each student. Create a sign-up sheet so that no student is missed. Conduct conferences informally but take notes. With this system, you can keep records of your meetings and can monitor the progress of each student.

- **Cruise Conferences**—Circulate around the room. Look through each writing folder, review the work in progress, staple samples to the folder, record grades, etc. This can be accomplished in just a few minutes at each work area. This method helps keep all students on task because they know their folders are checked regularly.

- **Student-initiated Conferences**—Set aside a time for students to come to you for help or with questions about their writing. You could use the "take a number" system. *Example:* If you have a 40-minute writing block, you can see eight students for 5 minutes each (numbers 1 through 8).

- **Combination Conferences**—Rotate periods of assigned, student-initiated, and cruise conferences.

Managing the Conference

A writing program that includes productive conferences with each student requires efficient use of time. Here are some tips for managing conference time.

- Focus on the writing process. Ask open-ended questions that lead your students to self-assessment. Check spelling, grammar, etc., especially when their work is in progress.

- Look for missing sections or ideas in the work. Ask students to explain what they intend to say, then show them how to incorporate the ideas into their work.

- Teach skills in the context of your student's writing. Keep grade-level appropriate writing samples on hand to illustrate such skills as indenting paragraphs, putting conversation in quotes, and making nouns and verbs agree.

Communication

• As you look at students' writing, take note of the skills with which several or all of your students may need help. Form an instructional group to teach or reteach individual skills as needed.

• Use a portion of the conference time for positive reinforcement of progress, even if it seems minimal. Try to make a written comment on the work. If the work is in progress, note where your conference left off and the date. At the student's next conference, you can skim to that point.

• Be sure to spend conference time with each student on a regular basis. Make every effort to give that student your complete attention during his time.

Conference Questions

During conferences with students, your questions should lead them to reflect on their works in progress. At the right is a list of questions that you may want to ask.

1. Tell me about your writing.
2. What gave you this idea?
3. How is your work going?
4. Are you stuck?
5. What were you thinking as you wrote this?
6. Where do you want to take this?
7. What do you mean by this?
8. What do you want your reader to think?
9. Who do you want to read this?
10. Have you read what you wrote aloud?
11. Have you read this to someone else?
12. Has one of your peers read this?
13. Are you pleased with what you have written?
14. Do you want to make any changes now?
15. What can you do differently now?
16. What can you do with this part?
17. How can I help you?
18. Do you want to add anything to this?
19. What do you plan to do next?
20. Do you want to publish this?

EDITING THE WORK

Everyone would like to write a polished piece in one attempt, but impress upon your students that even "professional" writers revise during the writing process. Try these techniques:

Suggestions

• Base your revision expectations on the work, your student's skill level, and the complexity of the piece.

• Let your students know that some, but not all, of their writings may need to be edited and rewritten. Let students categorize their writings in a classification system to identify the purpose of each work. *Examples:* Personal, Practice, Assignment, Enjoyment, or Publication. Explain that only writing that is for an assignment or for publication will have to go through the entire writing process.

• Developing writers need a balance between editing pieces and getting on with the next creation. A good policy to follow is to polish work intended for publication and to set aside the rest in draft form in the writing folder. The drafts should be considered works "in progress." They are worth keeping for several months if only to track your students' writing skills growth.

• Model revisions using your own writing. Think out loud and discuss problems you are facing, changes you need to make, and possible alternatives. Enlist your students' help in deciding what to revise. Let them see that there are many ways to revise a piece. Show them that a work in progress may have cross-outs, notes, sentences in the margins, and arrows that reorganize paragraphs, omissions, and inserts. If you teach students that completing and polishing a paper involves several important stages, they will be more receptive to making revisions.

Rule of Thumb

A good rule of thumb: Develop a peer-editing system. Train your students to be supportive readers of each other's works in progress. A peer editor should offer constructive criticism, check punctuation and grammar, and serve as a sounding board for the author.

Editing Partners or Teams

Realistically, you cannot correct and grade all the written work of a productive group of students, especially students who are writing every day. Establishing editing partners or teams in your learning environment will provide much-needed support. These "student editors" confer with their peers and help each prepare their work for publication. Peer review has many advantages:

Suggestions

• It creates a real audience for your students' work.

• Students learn from one another's experiences.

• Children begin to write for each other, not for an adult.

• It inspires writers to work more carefully.

Teach your students these common proofreading marks.

ℓ	take out extra letters or words	havᵉing
≡	change to a capital letter	john ≡
/	change to a lowercase letter	on my Ḥat
∧	put in missing letters or words	Weᵈnesday
⊙	add a period	Sit down⊙
⌄	insert a comma	After that ⌄
⌄	insert an apostrophe	can't
SP	check spelling	becawse SP
¶	begin a new paragraph or indent	¶ Once there
⌄⌄	insert quotation marks	"I should go swimming," he said.

PUBLISHING THE WORK

Ideas

Nothing will spark a student's desire to write as much as the prospect of sharing the work with an audience. Publication gives an importance to writing that assignments prepared for grades alone do not.

There are many ways to make your students' work public. In the writing process approach, publishing is not limited to the traditional definition but rather encompasses a variety of ways to share the work with others (see page 37). The form that publishing a particular work takes depends on the work and the goals of the writer. Here is a list of publishing ideas to consider:

- Create a class or school newspaper. Assign student reporters, editors, etc.

- Encourage students to enter writing contests found in children's magazines.

- Highlight a student author of the week on a bulletin board.

- Make individual or group books.

- Ask students to present written stories as plays.

- Establish an overnight check-out system so students can read classmates' research reports at home.

    - Help students prepare and send letters to authors, thank-you letters, and letters of inquiry.

    - Ask students to make dictionaries, handbooks, or other booklets for children in lower grades.

    - Challenge students to write group chain-novels. (Students add to a story started by another.)

    - Make an audio or video recording of an author's presentation.

- Let students set a piece of writing to music.

- Start a pen-pal program with another class.

- Invite students to create a mural showing the setting of a work to use as a backdrop for reading the work aloud.

Writing

WRITING ACTIVITIES

Every piece of writing should have a purpose, such as to inform, persuade, describe, or entertain. Try these activities to teach and inspire your students to write:

Creative Writing

- Help your students learn to sequence ideas. Assign a partner to each student. Give the pair a copy of a paragraph in which the sentences are written separately in mixed sequence. Instruct them to cut the sentences apart and rearrange them in a clear, logical order. Look for examples of your students' work to use in reinforcement lessons or to teach related skills, such as combining sentences with connector words (conjunctions).

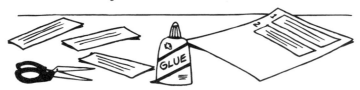

- Introduce descriptive writing. Tell students that writing a description is like painting a picture with words. Teach or review types of words that lend themselves to descriptive writing: colorful adjectives, sensory words, similes, and metaphors. Ask students to write three sensory words or a phrase describing how something looks, sounds, smells, feels, and tastes. Next, give each student a picture. Ask the students to write descriptions based on their pictures. Instruct them to write their stories as if no one else had seen the pictures. Tell the students to use lots of details and sensory words to describe objects, characters, or action.

Essay Writing

Writing

- Help each student organize an informal essay. Instruct the students to choose topics with three parts, such as "My Three Pets." Tell them each to write five paragraphs. The first should introduce the topic and the three parts. The next three paragraphs should give details about each part. The final paragraph should offer a summary or conclusion.

- Help students write persuasive essays. Begin by asking them to write down things they would like to see changed at home. Next, tell them to list things they would like to see changed in their learning environments. Tell them each to choose one item for the topic. To prepare for writing, tell them to list the reasons why a change is needed and details of how a change should be made. When they are ready to write, challenge them to try to convince you to share their points of view.

Journal Writing

- Have your students keep writing journals for jotting down ideas, thoughts, interesting words, spelling helps, phrases, strong active verbs, examples, etc. Their journals can also contain samples of various writing activities.

- Test each student's memory skills with this journal-writing activity. Ask the student to think back to the earliest experience she recalls clearly. How old was she? Have her write about this memory in her journal with as much detail as she can.

Ideas

- Take a moment to let students close their eyes and daydream. Get them started by telling them to imagine a place—how it looks, how it feels, how it smells. Then tell them to let a story unfold in that place. After a period of silence, have students write a journal entry titled "Lost in a Daydream." Instruct them to write down as many details as they can about the dream's setting, characters, and events. They should record any conversations they imagined, and tell how the daydream made them feel.

Rule of Thumb

A good rule of thumb: Have each student keep two separate journals—one for drafts, works in progress, and journal entries you will ask to see, and another for personal reflection that is for their eyes only. Assure the students that you will respect their privacy with regard to personal journal entries.

Letter Writing

- Instruct your students in the finer points of letter writing. Show them the heading, salutation, body, closing, and signature for each letter form. Give them practice writing several types: friendly letters, thank-you letters, invitations, pen-pal letters, business letters, research-by-mail letters, fan letters, editorials, letters of complaint, and cover letters. All of these activities can help students appreciate the many varieties of this writing form.

Poetry Writing

Ideas

- Encourage poetry writing by offering poem-starters—once rhythmic line from a poem (famous or original) on which to build. Begin by brainstorming several lists of rhyming words. Then ask your students to choose and complete a poem starter, such as "I think that I shall never see . . . ," "Once upon a midnight dreary . . . ," or "Did I ever tell you about the time . . . ?"

- Teach your students how to write acrostic poems. Ask them to write their names vertically in capital letters, then create poems by using each letter to begin a line. *Tip:* Remind students that not all poetry has to rhyme!

Example of an acrostic poem by Sara:

Someday I'll be a famous Actress. I'll play all sorts of Roles. Sometime I'll win an Academy Award!

Journalistic Writing

- Invite your students to be "cub reporters." Begin by giving this assignment: A spaceship has landed nearby. Write a news report that tells who, what, where, when, and how; then illustrate your scoop.

- Help your students create a mini-newspaper. Teach them the aspects of publishing the news—gathering facts, taking notes, doing interviews, writing stories, creating illustrations, writing headlines, planning layout, and printing.

EVALUATING WRITING

An effective monitoring system is essential to a well-designed writing program. Ongoing evaluation enables you to individualize writing instruction for your students and helps you assess their progress. Consider incorporating these features into your evaluation procedures:

Evaluation

- **Record-Keeping System**—Establish a planned system in which individual folders or portfolios are maintained with representative samples of each student's work.

- **Checklists**—Create a checklist of skills, concepts, and writing steps. Include a scoring system you can use to identify your students' needs and areas of growth.

- **Diagnostic System**—Design brief objective tests to pinpoint mechanical, structural, and usage errors.

- **Format Coverage Log**—Keep a log that tracks students' exposure to and experience with various types of writing—narrative, expository, and creative.

- **Focused-Feedback Assignments**—Give writing assignments that focus on a specific writing skill or concept. Evaluate the composition on only that skill.

- **Peer Evaluation**—Instruct your students to read and critique each other's writing, then discuss the papers. This can be done as partners or in small cooperative groups.

- **Instructor-Student Conferences**—Schedule time daily to meet with your students to discuss their works in progress, writing projects, and practice efforts. Prepare questions that encourage self-evaluation.

Rule of Thumb

A good rule of thumb: Portfolios are powerful assessment tools. Well-managed, organized portfolios present a broad picture of each student's individual strengths and weaknesses and are an excellent tool for communicating with parents.

Writing Evaluation Checklist

Name: _____

Writing Project: _____

Date: _____

Draft: _____

Evaluation

	Yes!	Recheck	Needs Review
Ideas are clear and well-presented.			
Ideas follow the subject.			
Ideas are sequenced and in order.			
There are a variety of sentences.			
Vocabulary is broad and descriptive.			
Words are used correctly.			
Spelling is checked and corrected.			
Capitalization rules are followed.			
Punctuation is used correctly.			
Handwriting is neat.			

Comments: _____

_____

_____

Grade: _____ (if applicable)

Planning a Great Science Fair Project

Help your students discover the joys and wonder of scientific investigation! This chapter offers practical ideas, tips, and steps for guiding your students through the science fair process, from choosing a topic to presenting the project at the fair. There are also easy to implement ideas that will make sharing the experience of scientific investigation fun and rewarding for both you and your students.

SCIENCE FAIR OBJECTIVES

Suggestions

Exposing elementary-age students to a variety of scientific experiences at home and at school increases the likelihood that they will develop positive attitudes toward science. In this spirit, a science fair program should include the following objectives:

- Encourage inquiry. Teach students how to ask questions and look for ways to solve problems.

- Teach students to value open-mindedness. Help them learn how to respond when an experiment does not work.

- Develop resourcefulness. Help students learn how and where to find information and assistance.

- Promote self-reliance. Help students learn how to investigate problems on their own.

As students develop these skills and attitudes while preparing for a science fair, they are also acquiring a scientific way of looking at the environment that will be useful throughout their lives.

THE SCIENTIFIC METHOD

In using the scientific method, students will observe, use scientific language, sharpen critical thinking skills, practice problem solving, record data, and draw conclusions.

PURPOSE
1. State the problem.
2. Form a hypothesis. (What will happen?)
PROCEDURE
3. Take steps to prove or disprove hypothesis.
4. Perform the experiment. (Observe and test.)
RESULTS
5. Record results. (What actually happened?)
CONCLUSION
6. State your conclusion.
(What discoveries did you make?)

CHOOSING A TOPIC

Steps to Take

Helping your students select a topic for investigation does not have to be an overwhelming experience. By following the simple activities listed below, you can steer them in the right direction—toward a topic of real scientific interest.

Brainstorming: First try brainstorming to get the ideas flowing. This technique generates many varied thoughts! Keep these rules in mind:

• Assign someone to record the ideas.

• Accept every suggestion—zany ones, too.

• Continue until there are many ideas—the more the better!

• Piggyback ideas—one idea sparks another.

When you have a long list of ideas, review each one to determine if it should be considered or eliminated. Make notes beside some, cross out some, and circle any that seem to be of particular interest. *Example:*

weather—may be too broad

~~gravity~~—not very practical

(Why do leaves change color?)

Webbing: Another way for students to develop ideas is to create a web—a graphic representation of topics and subtopics that relate to a main topic. Demonstrate how to expand this method of brainstorming by building a second web that extends from one idea or from a subtopic of the first idea.

Writing

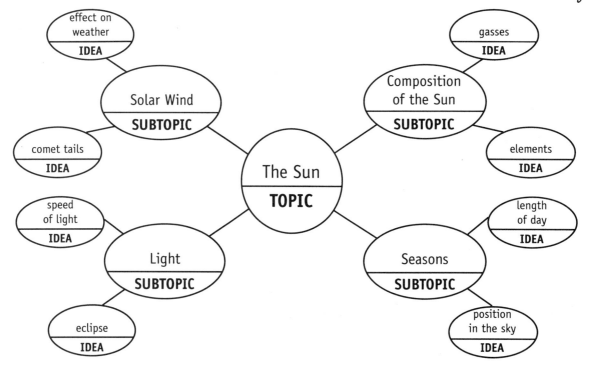

Ask students to choose one topic from the brainstorming or webbing activities. Challenge them to write ten questions about that topic. Discuss those questions, and ask them to focus on one question that they think would make a great science fair project.

Rule of Thumb

A good rule of thumb: At this level, a good science fair topic asks a question that can be answered by conducting an experiment. *Example*: How do pill bugs react to different surfaces?

Suggestions

Independent Activity: After practicing brainstorming and webbing techniques together, students can use these techniques independently to zero in on any subject of interest!

PLANNING THE PROJECT

The Purpose . . .

Investigation

After the student selects a topic to investigate, she needs to form a hypothesis. A hypothesis is a possible solution to a problem or a guess as to the outcome of a scientific inquiry.

Example:
Topic: What brand of popcorn pops the most kernels?
Hypothesis: Perfect-Pop Popcorn pops the most kernels.

The Procedure . . .

Once the student has formed a hypothesis, have him write out the steps he will take to prove or disprove it. The following list is an invaluable reference tool. It can serve both as a step-by-step guide for the students and as a progress-evaluation tool for you.

Steps to Take

1. What are the goals and objectives you are trying to accomplish? Describe the project in detail.

2. What resources will you need? List any books, magazines, or other sources you may use, including people you may need to contact.

3. What technical assistance will you require? List people who may be able to help you and in what way.

4. Who is your target audience? List the people who will see the project and those who will judge it.

5. What materials or special equipment will you need?

6. How do you envision the appearance of the final display? Draw a sketch.

Your enthusiasm plays a vital role in making the planning process go smoothly. If you encourage the students to search for different types of information, comment about interesting things they are discovering in compiling their material, and make different types of reference materials readily available, the science fair project planning process can be a great success.

RESEARCHING THE TOPIC

Investigation

When your students have completed the purpose and procedure, they are ready to investigate on their own.

No matter what the topic or purpose of the project, the first step is library research. Encourage your students to investigate books, periodicals, microfiche, vertical files, the card catalog, science texts, encyclopedias, filmstrips, videos, educational software, or perhaps conduct an Internet search for information on the topic.

Writing

Using index cards is an excellent method of recording and keeping the information the students find at the library. Show them how to record information on index cards for future use. Instruct them to write only one idea on each card.

For periodicals, include the date, volume number, and page numbers. *Example:* Carver, C. "Bugs Aren't Bad." *Scientific Discoveries* Vol. 3 (May 26, 1995): 34–35.

Your involvement at this stage can vary according to the ability levels of your students. Here are some additional ideas you may want to suggest as they conduct their research.

Suggestions

- Keep all materials in a dedicated science fair folder.
- Write letters to individuals or companies about the topic.
- Interview people who know a great deal about the topic.
- Make models or samples.
- Gather information by survey or questionnaire.
- Visit interesting places that might provide insight.
- Draw illustrations—visualizing enhances understanding.

CONDUCTING THE EXPERIMENT

Steps to Take

If your students have little or no experience conducting experiments, begin with a controlled experiment. This method encourages scientific discovery and can provide lots of fun for everyone. Start by asking your students questions that challenge them to explore their prior knowledge and future expectations. Then discuss what actions will be required to achieve the desired results.

- *What do I already know about this topic?*
- *What do I want to learn? What will the experiment show?*
- *What steps must I take to complete my experiment?*

Variables . . .

In any experiment there are variables—things that change or cause a change in the process or the results. Some variables can be controlled, others cannot. Direct students toward experiments in which the variables can be controlled.

Suggestions

In an experiment, the investigator changes the variables in order to observe what will happen. This "IF . . . THEN . . ." approach is one of simple cause and effect.

There are two types of variables in an experiment: independent and dependent. The *independent variable* is the thing the experimenter changes—the cause. The resulting action is the *dependent variable*. It "depends" on what the experimenter does—the effect.

Showing students how to control these variables is easy—have them designate one group as an *experimental group* and another as the *control group*.

To illustrate, share the following example of a simple controlled experiment set-up with your students.

SAMPLE CONTROLLED EXPERIMENT SETUP

Topic:
Does *GrowPlus Fertilizer* affect the growth of bean plants? (*GrowPlus* is an imaginary chemical fertilizer.)

Possible Variables:
• light source
• amount of water received
• type of soil planted in
• size of container grown in
• temperature
• location where grown

Test Plan:
Grow 20 bean plants. To be confident about the experiment, all the variables above will be the same (controlled) for all the plants. Then, ten of the bean plants will be given GrowPlus Fertilizer. These are the *experimental group*. The other ten will not receive fertilizer, so they are the *control group*. Other than the fertilizer variable, all plants will receive the same treatment.

RECORDING DATA AND RESULTS

The Results . . .

Writing

How do you assist students in the organization of data? Guide them by suggesting they answer these questions:

• *What happened in my experiment?*

• *How will I report the data? (graphs, tables, notes . . .)*

• *Why did I get these results? (This happened because . . .)*

• *Did my prediction match the results? Why or why not?*

• *If I did the experiment again, what would I do differently?*

Word Data: If their observations are in the form of words, instruct the students to make neat, written records or charts of everything they do. Encourage them to log all observations concerning their experimentation. (The computer is also a useful logging tool.)

Rule of Thumb

A good rule of thumb: Instruct students to include their experiment logs as part of their visual displays!

OBSERVATIONS AND DATA		
Date	Control Group	Experimental Group

Number Data: If the results are in numbers, suggest that the students organize their observations in the form of graphs—easy-to-see visual displays of data. Have them choose the form most appropriate to their data: bar graph, line graph, or circle graph.

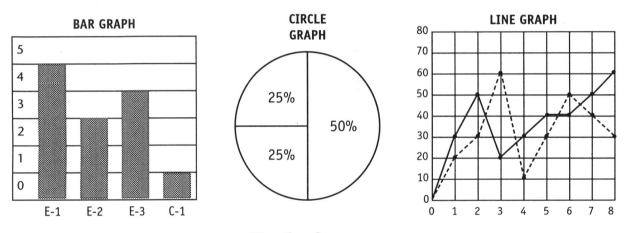

The Conclusion . . .

Finally, the young scientist is ready to draw a conclusion from her experimentation. Ask her to write a paragraph explaining what the findings prove or disprove. Did her observations match her predictions?

WRITING THE RESEARCH PAPER

The scientific research paper is an important part of the total project. The following steps will help guide students toward creating orderly papers worthy of presentation.

Rule of Thumb

A good rule of thumb: To keep it manageable, instruct the student to focus on one section of the paper at a time.

1. **Abstract**—Includes all applicable information: name, address, town, school, age or grade, category of project, followed by three short paragraphs explaining the purpose, procedure, and results.

2. **Title Page**—Displays the title of the project in the center; personal information (name, etc.) appears in the bottom right corner.

Steps to Take

3. **Table of Contents**—Lists the sections of the paper and the page on which each begins.

4. **Purpose**—States the project's purpose in three sentences or less.

5. **Acknowledgments**—Expresses thanks to everyone who contributed to the project.

6. **Body**—Reports on the research done and gives facts that introduce the subject. (This is the time to use those index cards!)

7. **Procedure**—Explains the experiment step by step and lists all of the materials used. Include drawings, if any, on separate pages in this section.

8. **Results**—Gives logs, graphs, and charts of data.

9. **Conclusion**—Evaluates and interprets results relative to the purpose stated. (Use your data to draw a conclusion about what has been proved or disproved. Do not be afraid to admit mistakes. Negative results are not bad; if your results did not prove your hypothesis, say so.)

10. **Bibliography**—Lists books, articles, and other sources used in research. List references in alphabetical order by author. *Example for book title:* Jones, John. *A Study of Plant Life.* New York: Wingate Publishing Company, 1994.

DESIGNING THE VISUAL PRESENTATION

A visual display is a great way of presenting the project to others. As with all parts of the science fair project, encourage students to take the time to plan their displays carefully. Have each student follow these steps:

Design

1. Design a backboard from sturdy materials. It should be able to stand by itself on a tabletop. Pre-made cardboard display boards are available at many teacher supply/parent resource stores.

2. Choose colors for the display. Paint the backboard or cover it in fabric or bright paper. Display the title of the project prominently in large cutout letters in contrasting colors.

3. Mount, tack, or pin all the elements of the science project to the backboards. Use your imagination to make your design appealing. Include such things as photos, charts, drawings, and diagrams large enough for the viewer to see easily.

4. Design a report folder with a cover that will interest the reader in the project.

Rule of Thumb

A good rule of thumb: Once the student has decided what will go on the backboard, have him lay the whole thing out on the floor and evaluate the arrangement before mounting the pieces.

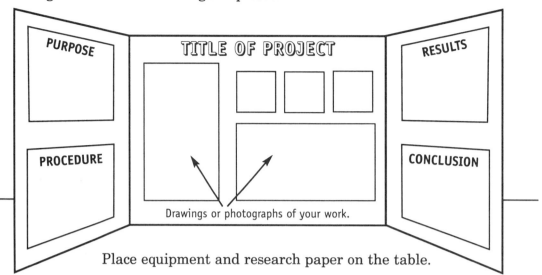

PURPOSE

TITLE OF PROJECT

RESULTS

PROCEDURE

CONCLUSION

Drawings or photographs of your work.

Place equipment and research paper on the table.

PLANNING THE ORAL PRESENTATION

Steps to Take

The oral presentation for the judges is a very important part of the project. Practice will make the difference in how well your students present themselves. Encourage them to rehearse in front of a mirror, and then later make a practice presentation before a "live" audience—you, a friend, or someone else who will listen attentively. The following steps may be a helpful guide for students.

1. Make introductions. First, introduce yourself. "Hello. My name is ___." Next, introduce the project. "The title of my project is __." Then, introduce the purpose. "The purpose of my project is ___." Finally, introduce your procedure. "The procedure I followed was ___."

2. Show your results. If you have a log, charts, or graphs, show them to the judges. If they are on the display, point them out and explain each.

3. Explain your conclusion. If you feel you had some problems with experimentation, do not be afraid to talk about them. Even the best scientists have to overcome obstacles along the road to discovery.

4. Discuss what you learned. Tell what you discovered about the topic or about the scientific process itself. Explain what you would do differently if you were to repeat this experiment or conduct another.

5. Invite questions. Ask the judges if they have any questions or items they would like explained further.

6. Say thank you! Do not forget to thank your listeners for their attention and interest.

Rule of Thumb

A good rule of thumb: Remind students to display good manners: Stand up straight to the side of the exhibit; look listeners in the eye; avoid chewing gum or candy; be polite; and, of course, SMILE!

EVALUATING THE PROJECT

Evaluation

Here are a few strategies you can use to evaluate the efforts of your students.

- Hold conferences with individual students at different stages of the project. This provides you with feedback on each student's effort, quality of work, and mastery of research skills.

- Encourage each student to do a periodic self-evaluation. This lets you gauge how the students rate their own efforts. One way to do this is to have them answer "yes" or "no" and explain their answers to questions such as these:

  1. I spent the right amount of time on this task.

  2. My project is well-planned and organized.

  3. I understand my topic and what I am doing.

  4. My project focuses on my original question.

  5. I am using enough sources of information.

  6. I am learning new information.

  7. My project shows creativity and problem solving.

- Final projects can be evaluated according to these criteria:

  1. Is the report complete? Are all of the components present, organized, and concisely written?

  2. Do the project components (written report, display, model, etc.) reflect an understanding of the topic?

  3. Does the project address the hypothesis, give evidence of experimental research, and exhibit use of the scientific method?

  4. Does the project display creativity, originality, and neatness?

A WORD ABOUT AWARDS

It is important to instill in your students a healthy view of competition. Winning is terrific, but it is not the most important part of a science fair project. The enjoyment of working on the project, conducting the experiments, exhibiting the work, and discovering science should be the primary reasons for participating in a science fair.

Remind your students that judges are human—and as such, each has a unique perspective. Their view may be different from yours. Even if you think the project is perfect, the judges may see ways it could be improved. This may be difficult for some students to accept, but it is part of the process.

Urge your students to listen carefully to the judges' critique and learn from it.

Finally, let students know that each of them is a "winner" by having made the effort to participate. They discovered new things for themselves and deserve recognition! If participant awards are not automatically given to every student, you can make up your own!

Certificate
awarded to
Deborah Hanson
For: *Science Fair 1999*
Project: *Are Molds Plants?*
Date: *April 23, 1999*

Steps to Take

YOUR STEPS TO THE SCIENCE FAIR

Adapt this checklist to meet your specific needs.

Responsibilities	Due Date	✔
Select topic; get parent approval/signature.		
Write purpose; form a hypothesis.		
Make a list of materials needed.		
Write procedure; begin research.		
Prepare draft of purpose and procedure.		
Hold student/adult conference. 　　(check if all is on track)		
Begin experimentation; do safety check.		
Record data.		
Hold student/adult conference. 　　(experimentation checkpoint)		
Begin research paper.		
Prepare draft of cover and title page.		
Complete all pages specific to rules of science fair.		
Prepare draft of acknowledgement page.		
Prepare draft of bibliography page.		
Hold student/adult conference. 　　(checkpoint/results and conclusion)		
Prepare draft of results and conclusion.		
Prepare draft of table of contents and abstract.		
Draw, label, and organize charts and graphs.		
Edit research paper.		
Publish research paper.		
Prepare and organize visual display.		
Prepare speech note cards.		
Rehearse presentation.		

Reproducible Form

Strategies for a Multi-Age Group

A multi-age learning environment offers many advantages to the traditional classroom. This chapter outlines how you can take advantage of greater flexibility by employing an integrated curriculum and a variety of learning mediums. You will find strategies to help you structure your environment for optimum organization, management, and active learning within the multi-age group.

THE MULTI-AGE ADVANTAGE

Getting into Focus

Historically, multi-age education was the norm and students attended classes in a one-room schoolhouse out of necessity. Today, educators have discovered that a modernized version of this approach to learning has many advantages.

Multi-age learning environments are characterized by students of various ages and abilities working in different groups and in nontraditional ways. This approach encourages students to take responsibility for their own learning and gives them more freedom to progress at their own rates and at their own levels.

As as instructor in a multi-age learning environment, you have greater flexibility in how you group and teach your students. You can tailor lessons and activities to the ways your students learn best. You can assume the role of coach and mentor rather being a person who provides all the answers. Multi-age education employs an integrated curriculum and calls for a variety of learning mediums—learning centers, cooperative learning activities, and individualized instruction.

Multi-age education has the following advantages:

- Students are expected and encouraged to learn at different levels and rates. This reduces unnecessary competition and lessens academic failures.

- There are frequently fewer discipline problems because students are accepted and supported at their current stage of development.

- Multi-age instruction fosters cooperative learning. Older students gain self-esteem by acting as role models for younger learners. Younger learners benefit from exposure to "experienced" students.

- Students for whom English is a second language benefit from cooperative multi-age learning through extended opportunities to interact with a variety of students.

Rule of Thumb

A good rule of thumb: Remember, few, if any, adults spend their days working with people who are of the same age and ability—and there is no reason to expect a group of children to be any different. Diversity in the workplace, and in the learning environment, can be an advantage!

TEAMING UP TO TEACH

Ideas

Providing appropriate instruction for all students in a multi-age learning environment can be challenging. Such tasks as preparing individualized curricula, creating an organizational plan that works well for the entire group, and keeping the educational process running smoothly take careful planning, organization, and vigilance.

One way to manage the many responsibilities of multi-age instruction is to share them through team teaching. Home instructors can join with other parents and divide the teaching responsibilities for all their children. Traditional classroom teachers can share multi-age instruction through cross-grouping for certain subjects or activities. Whatever your learning environment, teaming up to teach can benefit you, your colleagues, and your students. Consider these benefits of team teaching:

- **Greater versatility and originality of presentations.** By working together and sharing all educational tasks, each of you can devote more energy to applying your particular strengths and talents to the program.

- **Flexibility in the grouping of your children.** You and your teaching partner can group and regroup your students to better meet instructional needs.

- **Time to give more individualized help.** You can organize your time so that one person is freed up to work with individuals while the other works with the groups.

- **Support and feedback on methods and practices.** Your partner can observe the effectiveness of your teaching, as well as the achievement and growth of your students.

THE MULTI-AGE ENVIRONMENT

Steps to Take

The use of space in a multi-age learning environment should be flexible. It should incorporate a number of learning zones and be supplied with a wide variety of easily accessible materials. The diagram on the following page and these steps will help you set up your multi-age environment.

1. Provide as much space as possible and divide it into functional areas or learning zones. *Example:* A corner of the room is designated and labeled "The Social Studies Zone."

2. Structure your environment around themes and integrate learning across content areas within the theme. *Example:* Within the theme of "Rain Forest," a young student can be working on the *ai* sound, while an older student is graphing the daily depletion of the rain forest.

3. Supply a wide selection of materials—art supplies, rulers, pictures, and manipulatives as well as print material. *Tip:* You will not need class-size sets of everything since most activities will involve only a few students at a time.

4. Provide a variety of "real books" that represent all the reading levels in your group. Include fiction, nonfiction, poetry, biographies, and so on.

5. Assign certain activities as requirements, but also allow your students to explore the room freely and choose activities individually or in groups.

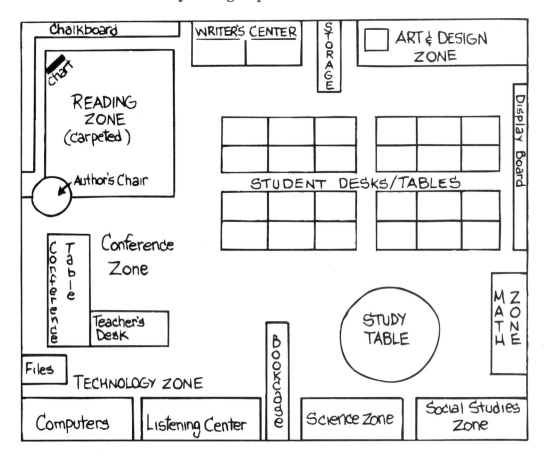

ORGANIZING FOR LEARNING

Suggestions

It is crucial to establish a consistent pattern of how the learning environment will operate on a day-to-day basis. Knowing what to expect in their multi-age learning environment will help all your students feel comfortable and enable them to begin each day on positive note. Follow these suggestions:

- Begin each day with a whole-group activity. This gives the group a sense of coherence and lets you set the tone. If necessary, review rules and procedures.

- Let older students occasionally cross-age tutor younger students. *Tip:* Do not overdo this or the older students will miss out on specific skills at their own level.

- When possible, teach music, art, and physical education to the whole group, then provide age-appropriate follow-up activities.

- Plan your program for a month at a time. Then each week do lesson plans in great detail, including step-by-step instructions for each student doing independent work.

- Create many cooperative learning group activities. Change the makeup of the groups often. Students can be grouped differently for different reasons. (See page 61.)

- Provide your students with many opportunities for independent study. Let them use library books, work at learning centers, keep journals, and research topics of interest.

- Create a learning activity timetable and post it. This will help keep you and your students organized and on task as you move through the day.

- Pair a student at the early stage of acquiring a skill with a student who is more adept but still needs practice. Allow an older student to check a younger one's work.

- Do not sort, track, or label students. A student can remain in a particular group until he has achieved mastery of the target skill and is ready to move on. Conversely, he need not remain in a particular group if he has mastered a skill. *Tip:* The objective is for a student to be neither pushed too fast nor held back by the group.

- Try sharing responsibilities with another teacher or parent if you have expertise in different areas.

- Establish weekly work plans or contracts to use with your students. These will also aid you in tracking and evaluating their progress.

- Enlist the aid of parents and friends in your learning environment. They can help directly by working with you and your students, or indirectly through donations of materials or at-home assistance.

Rule of Thumb

A good rule of thumb: Be cautious about how you correct older students in front of younger ones. Older students should be reminded that they are "mature" members of the learning community who can handle more responsibility. Your younger ones will look up to and emulate the older students, so be sure to preserve their influence as positive role models.

TEACHING SELF-DIRECTION

A student who can take charge of herself, make responsible choices, pursue her own interests, and learn without your constant supervision is likely to become a self-motivated, lifelong learner.

Steps to Take

If your students are to become self-directed learners, you must teach them to learn independently, just as you teach phonics to enable them to read.

To teach self-direction, start with activity choices that let your students do things they already know about and enjoy. Begin with the following step-by-step instructions:

1. Set up three to six activities in which your students can work on a task without direct supervision, such as doing puzzles or listening to stories at a listening center.

2. Describe the choices to your students, where they are located, and how many students can participate.

3. Give clear directions for selecting an activity, working appropriately, cleaning up when finished, and making another activity choice.

4. Direct each student to select an activity to do first.

5. Ask the students to model how to go to the activities or get materials for them. Then ask the students if they feel they are ready to do the activities without any help.

6. Dismiss your students a few at a time to make their choices, and direct them to begin.

7. Circulate for 15 to 20 minutes in order to diagnose your students—their needs, interests, and abilities to focus and sustain effort on the activities.

8. Hold a group discussion to evaluate the independent learning session. Ask students to comment on the experience and suggest how it might be improved.

9. Record the names of students who need help and note their areas of weakness.

10. Reinforce your students' productive behavior, such as gathering needed materials, focusing on a task, ignoring distractions, moving from one activity to the next, and cleaning up. This is a very important step, so be sure to praise all appropriate and positive actions.

11. Teach your students a signal that indicates that there are 2 to 3 minutes remaining before the close of an activity and time to clean up.

12. Teach another signal to indicate that it is time to stop, clean up, and return to a designated area for evaluation of their performance in working independently. Reinforce those who respond productively to the signal. *Example:* "You got a lot done today—you can work well on your own." Refocus and restart those students who did not sustain their effort. *Example:* "Show me what you will do next," or "What kept you from being able to complete this activity today? Let's see how we can help make sure you will able to complete it tomorrow."

13. Reteach the same procedure each day until it becomes routine. Now you can work with a small instructional group for a short time, while observing the self-direction of the rest of your students. Afterward, circulate again among the independent learners to reinforce their productive behavior.

14. Add new independent activities to the learning environment every week or so. As new activities are added, old ones should be removed so that your students neither lose interest nor face too large an assortment of choices.

15. Once your students have mastered working independently, provide creative contracts and assign job cards. *Tip:* For extra motivation, add a few activities designed or made by the students!

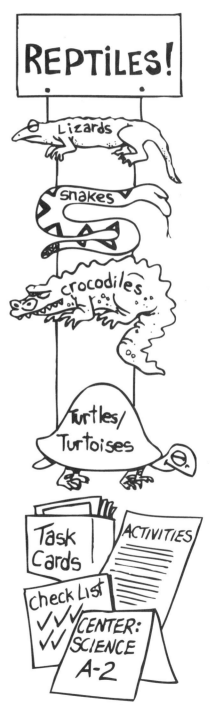

STRATEGIES FOR MULTI-AGE LEARNING

Ideas

Here is list of strategies and ideas to keep in mind as you strive for optimum results in your multi-age learning environment:

- Regard each student as an important individual with her own social, emotional, and intellectual needs. Start expecting the best from each student because, more often than not, you get only as much as you expect!

- Use a variety of methods to evaluate your students' progress—demonstrations, projects, essays, discussions, and explanations as well as tests and quizzes.

- Keep a portfolio of each student's work. Sometimes the work selected can be the student's choice and other times it will be your choice.

- Encourage your students to take risks in accomplishing tasks. Emphasize that we learn more from our mistakes than from perfect performances. *Tip:* Never criticize a student for failing at a task at which she made an honest effort. Instead, praise the effort and encourage her to try again.

- Give your students frequent feedback on their progress, but also seek feedback on your own performance from peers and parents and through self-evaluation.

- Teach your students to focus on doing the job well, rather than on competing with a fellow student.

- Interview your children to determine what they have learned. Ask older students to write progress reports listing their accomplishments, describing current projects, and stating their learning goals. This gives you valuable insight, gives your students a chance to reflect on their learning, and gives parents a concrete evaluation tool.

Rule of Thumb

A good rule of thumb: Students who are self-motivated often work for the inherent satisfaction of doing the task. They take risks, assume responsibility, solve problems, and work well in groups—all traits worth cultivating!

DIAGNOSING NEEDS

A primary goal of multi-age learning is to provide students with the opportunity to progress at their own rates. To do this, you must employ diagnostic teaching skills. Discover your students' strengths and weaknesses in all curriculum areas, then prescribe a program designed to capitalize on their strengths and improve their weaknesses. Each daily learning situation provides you with information you can use as a basis for grouping and individualizing your instruction.

Evaluation

Here are some ideas for gathering diagnostic data:

- Create a diagnostic information sheet. Include the student's name, age, grade level, medical data, achievement test scores and dates, patterns of behavior, interests, special talents, abilities, contributions, and achievements.

- Record observations about your students in a journal. Observations about a student's behavior in specific situations can help you predict the student's future reactions to given situations. Recorded anecdotal observations are an invaluable technique for diagnosing a student's needs and capabilities. They also provide a history of behavior patterns you can use to document opinions expressed in a report or conference.

- Create a check sheet for obtaining and recording information about each student's current level of performance. Not only can you learn from this information, but you can use it as a base from which to inform parents about their student's performance and progress.

- Encourage your students to evaluate themselves. This will help you find out where each student feels insecure or confident with the curriculum. A student's self-evaluation can be a powerful tool for communicating with parents.

- Give diagnostic tests to all of your students. Begin testing the student at the level at which you feel she will succeed. Then move to more difficult tests until you discover her general instructional level.

GROUPING YOUR CHILDREN

Planning

One key to success in a multi-age learning environment is the variety of groupings. These give your students the opportunity to advance at their own pace, tutor others, and mix with students of different ages, abilities, and interests. Try any or all of these groupings:

- **Problem-solving grouping**—Learners grouped around a common unsolved topic or problem. *Example:* A group formed to discuss and determine the main idea of a story.

- **Needs-requirement grouping**—Students are instructed in a concept, skill, or procedure. *Example:* A group is formed for instruction in parts of speech.

- **Reinforcement grouping**—Learners who need more work in a specific area or task. *Example:* A group formed to review how to convert fractions to decimals.

- **Interest grouping**—Learners who want to work on a project together. *Example:* A group formed to prepare a skit about the first steps taken on the moon.

- **Learning-style grouping**—Learners who have a common learning style. *Example:* A group formed to study place value by working with manipulatives.

Handling Group Conflict

Suggestions

In any group, conflicts occasionally arise. Tempers can flare before logical problem-solving occurs. Instruct your students to use the steps below to analyze a conflict and learn from it. Have them talk about or write down their reactions. With regular practice your students will use the strategy automatically.

STOP. (Everyone stop whatever you're doing.)

Silently count to 10. Then respond to these statements.

1. This is what happened.

2. This is what I did.

3. Here are three other ways I could have reacted.

4. This is what I could try next time.

COOPERATIVE LEARNING

Steps to Take

In forming cooperative learning groups, consider each student's strengths in the selected curriculum area, level of independence as a learner, skill at problem solving, and strength in group leadership and dynamics. You may consider other factors based on the task you plan to give the group. *Example:* If the group task involves producing a visual display, consider placing students with strong artistic abilities in different groups.

Follow these steps to implement a cooperative group activity.

1. Define the task to be accomplished. Hold a conference with the group to determine the process the group will use, the products they will produce, and a method for evaluating the process and products. Timelines, contracts, and individual responsibilities may be set at this time, or these decisions may be made later by the group.

2. Monitor the effectiveness of the cooperative learning group and intervene to provide task assistance (answering questions and teaching task skills) or to refocus the group if necessary.

3. Assess your students' skills by evaluating not only the group's product or results, but the process used. Ask each student to evaluate the group's performance—*How well did the group collaborate? What "snags" did you encounter and how did you overcome them? Are you pleased with what the group produced? Why or why not? If you were starting over, what would you do differently?*

Rule of Thumb

A good rule of thumb: Cooperative learning activities are not only well suited for multi-age groups, they are also an excellent way to help students who are from different cultural backgrounds, or who are different physically and in gender, develop an awareness and appreciation of individual diversity.

Cooperative Learning Activities

Documenting in detail the organization, procedures, and dynamics of structured cooperative learning is beyond the scope of this text. The following are activities you can use when students are grouped for learning.

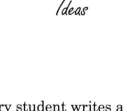

Ideas

- Create role cards for your students to use in cooperative learning groups. Under each role title, write a sentence describing the duties of the person holding that position in the group. Laminate the cards and reuse them throughout the year. Add cards as your students take on new projects. Make sure everyone in the group has an opportunity to play different roles: Reader, Questioner, Recorder, Editor, and so on.

- Direct each group to keep a group journal in which every student writes a sentence reflecting on the team experience—noting accomplishments and analyzing setbacks. *Tip:* Instead of using individual names, tell students to use *I, we,* and *the group.* Collect these journals to follow each group's progress.

- **Math**—Add team spirit to individual timed math tests. Place students in groups and average their individual scores to come up with a "team score." Challenge groups to beat their own team score with each new timed test given. Encourage them to celebrate their group's improvement, even if it is only a few points.

- **Spelling**—Give your students a basic spelling pretest. Tell each student to replace every correct word with a more challenging one from a special bonus list. (This results in a different spelling list for each student.) Form study groups for spelling. Have them study their lists in their groups and test each other at the end of the week. (You score this test.) Finally, instruct students to share strategies they learned in the group for remembering tricky words.

- **Reading**—Pair students as reading partners within a small reading discussion group. Present a topic to investigate. Ask each pair to read and discuss the topic, then share their findings or feelings with the group.

PEER POWER

Suggestions

Peer power simply means "learners helping learners." The concept is based on the old saying, "The best way to learn something is to teach it to someone else." Through peer power, students learn that they are part of a learning community in which they can rely on each other for support. In multi-age learning environments, students are encouraged to seek out peers for assistance. Here are just a few ways peer power can be used:

- Students can work together in interest groups on topics of their choice. *Tip:* Be sure to establish a goal and a method of evaluation beforehand.

- Students can be assigned to "buddy-projects" in which they pair up for a project or a period of time.

- Students can act as peer pals. (Involvement is primarily nonacademic.) Peer pals offer social and emotional support to new students, students who have missed activities, or students with physical handicaps. Their efforts can help give your students a sense of community and universal acceptance.

- Students can be appointed as "experts" on a subject for a period of time. When another student has a question or problem related to that subject, he can "ask the expert."

- Various students can be appointed "official ____" (timekeeper, assignment coordinator, homework helper, etc.) whom others can consult about organization, time management, and other nonacademic functions.

- Students who share a particular curriculum strength can act as "student mentors" to students who are having difficulties in that subject area (peer tutoring).

Rule of Thumb

A good rule of thumb: Students selected to act as peer tutors (from your learning environment or from another classroom) need to be trained, supervised, and evaluated for effectiveness. Be sure your peer tutors understand your expectations.

LEARNING CENTERS

Learning centers can be a valuable instructional tool in your multi-age learning environment. They give your students opportunities to develop self-direction and decision-making skills, as well as help them learn to work independently and to assume responsibility. Keep these points in mind as you plan and implement learning centers in your learning environment:

- There are many valid and successful ways to use learning centers. They can cover any subject area or concept you are teaching.

- Centers should be easy for you to establish, maintain, change, and evaluate.

- All of your students should have the opportunity to use the learning centers (though not necessarily every center).

- Center activities should reinforce, enrich, and extend your curriculum.

- State your expectations about behavior at the centers and set maximum numbers of students who can work at a center at one time. Hold a problem-solving discussion to evaluate work habits, behavior, or any problems involved in using the centers.

- Establish a simple, organized method of record-keeping for each center. The first few times your students use the centers, have them practice record-keeping as a group.

EVALUATING YOUR PROGRAM

Assessment is an important aspect of any instructional program. Assessment should always directly reflect what was taught and what was learned. The following steps will help you establish evaluation methods that assess students' progress and give you feedback on the effectiveness of your instruction.

Evaluation

Steps to Take

1. Clearly define for your students the purpose or goal of the learning activity. Recommend a plan for reaching the learning goal. Make sure your students understand your expectations and how their performances will be evaluated.

2. Define the goals in terms of observable behaviors. *Example:* "The student will be able to state three reasons for . . ." is better than "The student will learn about . . ." This allows your assessment to be objective rather than subjective. Create a checklist of goals and objectives. Share it with the students. *Example:* "At the end of the unit you will be able to name the 50 states and their capitals." *Tip:* You may want to share these objectives with parents so they can monitor their children's progress toward meeting them.

3. Do not wait until the end of an activity to assess progress. Identify checkpoints in which your students can share what they have learned and accomplished so far. Be observant and ready to step in and guide students as needed.

4. Collect evidence that your students are learning in the form of tests, quizzes, reports, essays, student-teacher conference notes, portfolios, tapes, etc.

5. Interpret the data you have gathered to evaluate the learning that has taken place and to determine where reteaching is necessary. If your students are experiencing difficulty, modify your teaching, or if necessary, modify the learning goal.

6. Rely on your students as co-evaluators of themselves, of their peers, and of you—their instructor. Their perspective will give you new insight!

Making Current Events Meaningful

You can show your students that history is being made every day! The study of current events teaches skills from across the curriculum and develops critical thinking and problem-solving abilities. This chapter includes activities and suggestions to help your students understand, analyze, and evaluate the events in the news and apply them to their lives.

WHY TEACH CURRENT EVENTS

Evaluation

Teaching current events is an important component of a balanced curriculum. It has obvious ties to social studies, but its scope reaches far beyond any one area of study. Here are some key reasons for teaching current events:
- Current events show students that history is being made every day.
- An understanding of current events helps create informed citizens.
- Current events demonstrate how the community works together and the challenges it faces.
- Current events supplement your health, science, and technology curriculum with up-to-date information.
- The study of current events makes students feel that they are a part of the world beyond themselves.
- Knowing how and where to find out about current events gives students the tools for lifelong learning.
- Current events offer a fresh and dynamic way to teach reading, writing, speaking, and listening skills.
- Studying current events involves critical thinking—analyzing, making inferences, identifying cause-and-effect relationships, applying information to new situations, synthesizing information, and evaluating pros and cons and facts and opinions.
- An awareness of current events—local, national, and international—gives students a new perspective on their place in the global community.

IMPLEMENTING YOUR PROGRAM

Evaluation

Just as there are countless teaching styles, there are a number of ways to implement a current events program. Choose one or more of the following approaches:

1. **Whole Class Instruction/Whole Class Activities**—The whole class studies the same news events and does the same follow-up activities.

2. **Whole Class Instruction/Independent Activities**—The whole class studies the same news events and students choose their own follow-up activities.

   Example: Everyone reads about a major local storm. One student graphs rainfall data, another conducts an interview, and a third student lists storm safety tips.

3. **Small Group**—Students work in small groups to analyze news events and create a group follow-up project. The teacher can choose the news events and activities for all groups to do or groups can choose their own project.

4. **Independent**—Each student works independently to choose, study, and complete follow-up activities for news events.

5. **Rotating**—Individuals, pairs, or groups are responsible for choosing news events to share with the class on a daily or weekly rotating basis.

Tip: No matter what strategies you choose to bring current events into your learning environment, teach your students to look and listen for key words in a news presentation. The steps given on page 68 for analyzing newspaper articles can be applied to any news source.

Rule of Thumb

A good rule of thumb: Begin teaching current events with whole class instruction. Once students know the process, move to the program that best fits your teaching style, or change the program throughout the year to keep it fresh for you and your students.

RESOURCES FOR NEWS

There are a number of resources available to you for teaching current events. Even if you choose to focus on only one source, it is valuable to expose students to a variety of resources so they can compare the format, style, and general features of each.

- **Newspaper**—This is a popular resource for use with groups of students—they can read it, write on it, cut it apart, and recycle it. Some newspapers offer special discounts and educational support materials to educators. Call your local newspaper. Tell them that you plan to use their paper as a teaching tool and ask what discounts or support materials they offer. *Tip:* Ask if the newspaper will send a representative to your learning environment as a guest speaker!

- **Children's news weeklies**—These provide a summary of the week's news written for students at different grade levels. *Examples: Weekly Reader* and *Scholastic News.* Call to ask for information concerning your specific needs—size of group and grade level(s).

- **News magazines**—These cover the week's most important national and international stories. *Examples: Time, Newsweek, U.S. News and World Report.* Some news magazines publish teacher guides and special student editions. *Note:* News magazines are most appropriate for older students.

- **Television**—Several local and national news programs are aired throughout the day.
- **Radio**—Some radio stations air both news summaries and feature programs.
- **Internet**—This computer resource lets students access news from a variety of sources throughout the world.

Rule of Thumb

A good rule of thumb: Have students watch television news with an adult. Some news stories feature visual images that can be disturbing. Students need to be able to talk about what they see immediately.

CHOOSING A FOCUS

A current events program can integrate many aspects of learning. It is important to choose a focus for current events activities, such as learning more about a science or a social studies topic you are studying or reinforcing a language skill. Change the focus to cover the key goals you want to accomplish. Here are some ideas:

Investigation

Themes—Choose a theme you are studying and have students look for current information about it. *Examples:*

- Elections
- Environment
- Space
- Transportation
- Weather
- Olympics
- Careers

Tip: Provide or have students come up with prompt questions to launch the search. *Example:* What is the most important issue in this election?

Skills—Use current events to teach a specific skill.

- Persuasive writing
- Reading maps and graphs
- Public speaking
- Reading for meaning— identifying the main idea

Critical Thinking—Ask students to think about a question, and then look in the news for facts that support their opinions. *Examples:*
- How is our state (province, country, continent) like other states? How is it different?
- What are children throughout the world experiencing?
- What is the greatest challenge our community faces?
- How is the earth's surface changing?
- What makes someone a leader?
- What are different ways of solving problems?

INTRODUCING THE NEWSPAPER

Begin by ordering a classroom set of newspapers for a certain day of the week. Then follow the steps below.

Rule of Thumb

A good rule of thumb: Many newspapers have expanded sections on specific days. Examples: Monday—business; Tuesday—science; Wednesday—food. Choose the day that best matches your educational focus.

1. Let students skim through their papers independently for 15 minutes. Direct them to circle with a crayon/marker any headlines, articles, pictures, or comics that appeal to them.

2. Point out that your newspaper is organized by sections (A, B, C; I, II, III; etc.). If your newspaper has an index, teach students where it is and how to use it.

3. Introduce each section of the newspaper and familiarize students with the information found there. As you review it, encourage students to discuss items they circled within each section.

Steps to Take

Children Send Care Packages by Luis Romero

Children at Harriet Tubman School are boxing toys and clothes for victims of

Charlotte, North Carolina fifth graders helped the

4. Teach students these newspaper terms and have them find examples:
   - Headline—the large words above an article that summarize the story
   - Byline—the name of the person who wrote the story
   - Dateline—the place listed at the beginning of a news story that tells from where the story comes
   - Cutline or Caption—a brief description below a photograph

TEACHING ABOUT NEWS STORIES

News stories are the backbone of a current events program. Have students follow these steps to locate and read an article.

Steps to Take

1. **Scan the headlines to choose a story.**
   The headline gives the main idea of a news story. If it is light news rather than hard (serious) news, the headline may use humor or a play on words.

2. **Skim the lead.**
   The lead is the first paragraph of the story. In a hard news story, it contains the most important facts. In a magazine article, a lighter news story, or a feature article about a program or person, the lead may be written in a style to catch the interest of the reader.

3. **Read the article.**
   The remainder of the article expands on the story. Read carefully to find details of importance or interest. Highlight or make notes of the answers to the 5 W's (explained on the following page).

The 5 W's

Investigation

A news story usually answers the 5 W's—*who, what, where, when,* and *why*—within the lead. The remainder of the article further explains the story's *how* and *why*.

Group Activity: Divide the class into groups of five. Assign each student within the group a different *W*. Have the group choose an article and each group member identify his or her *W* in the lead.

Individual Activity: Have students highlight each W in a news story's lead with a different color crayon or highlighter:

Who—red
What—blue
Where—green
When—yellow
Why—orange

TEACHING ABOUT EDITORIALS

Suggestions

An editorial expresses the viewpoint of an individual or a group at a newspaper, magazine, radio station, or television station. To understand an editorial, students must be familiar with the issue it addresses and be able to think critically about it. Analyzing editorials is a sophisticated skill that should be reserved for older students who have demonstrated higher level thinking abilities. *Tip:* Before teaching students about editorials, make sure that they understand the difference between fact and opinion. If necessary, do some review activities.

Begin teaching about editorials with a simple, easy-to-understand example. Read all or part of the editorial to the entire group, then help students analyze it with questions such as these:
- *What topic or issue does this editorial address?*
- *Which statements are facts?*
- *Which statements are opinions?*
- *How do the facts support the writer's opinions?*
- *What facts might have been left out?*
- *What is the author's purpose in writing the editorial?*
- *Who might agree with this editorial? Why?*
- *Who might disagree with this editorial? Why?*

Give students the opportunity to practice analyzing an editorial in cooperative learning groups. Have each group choose an editorial and answer the questions above. Ask a spokesperson from each group to report on how the group arrived at its answers and what, if any, problems arose during the process.

Rule of Thumb

A good rule of thumb: When students are first learning to read editorials, have them highlight facts with a yellow crayon and opinions with an orange crayon.

TEACHING ABOUT EDITORIAL CARTOONS

Suggestions

An editorial cartoon is a pictorial statement of a cartoonist's opinion. Understanding an editorial cartoon requires greater skill than understanding a regular editorial. Students must be able to identify the person or topic that is the subject of the cartoon, know the background news events that relate to it, and recognize the cartoon's message with few or no verbal clues. Again, reserve analyzing editorial cartoons for older students, and be sure to give plenty of guided practice before asking students to analyze editorial cartoons on their own.

Cartoonists use different styles to project their messages. Introduce one or more of these styles to students. If possible, provide an example of each.

- **Caricature**—Uses exaggeration or distortion of a person or symbol.
- **Satire**—Uses ridicule or wit to show foolishness or evil.
- **Symbolism**—Uses symbols to show objects, events, or relationships.
- **Literary allusion**—Uses familiar words from books, music, or films.
- **Pathos**—Stirs feelings of sympathy or compassion.

Rule of Thumb

A good rule of thumb: Always be on the lookout for editorial cartoons in newspapers and magazines. Start a file of those which students can understand and enjoy.

TEACHING ABOUT LETTERS TO THE EDITOR

Letters to the editor give readers the opportunity to respond to articles and editorials. In local newspapers they often provide a forum for debate about current issues. Follow these steps to introduce your students to letters to the editor.

Steps to Take

1. **Discuss—Why write a letter to the editor?**
   Brainstorm reasons why someone might write a letter to the editor. Supplement your list with these reasons:
   - To show that one agrees with a news story or editorial
   - To show that one disagrees with a news story or editorial
   - To give a differing viewpoint of events reported
   - To point out the inaccuracies in a news story
   - To address a story not reported

2. **Read letters to the editor.**
   Give students these pointers as you teach them to read letters to the editor critically:
   - Letters to the editor are opinions.
   - Information represented as facts within a letter may not be true. *(However, most publications would not knowingly print false statements.)*
   - Usually authors must take responsibility for their letters by giving their names and home-towns or addresses.

3. **Write letters to the editor.**
   Here are tips for writing letters to the editor:
   - Write a letter when you feel strongly about an issue.
   - Effective letters are clear, concise, and sincere.
   - As with anything that may be published, proofread your writing carefully.

Writing

COMMUNITY CONNECTIONS

Suggestions

In every community there are people who can augment your current events program. Try these ideas for tapping those resources.

Guest Speakers

Bring current events directly into your learning environment by inviting members of the community to be guest speakers.
- Reporters from a newspaper, magazine, radio station, or television station.
- People directly involved in a news event.
- People with background information regarding a news event. *(Example:* Invite a scientist who could explain how a new telescope is being launched into space.)

Field Trips

Let your students examine current events topics "in the field" with an on-site trip.
- Tour a newspaper plant, or a radio or television station.
- Take a trip to the scene of an important news event.
- Visit a museum with a collection that corresponds to a topic you are studying.

Projects Outside the Classroom

Challenge your students to expand their learning environment to encompass the whole community.
- Conduct a neighborhood survey to identify community support for or opposition to an issue.
- Interview someone directly involved in a news event.

FOLLOW-UP PROJECTS

Here are ways an individual, pairs, or groups of students can analyze, evaluate, or present what they learn.

Writing

Writing

- Write a new headline for a news story you read.
- List what you think are the three most important news events this week (month) and explain your reasoning.
- Glue a news story to a piece of paper. Copy and finish this sentence below it: "I think children should know about this news story because ____."
- Write three questions you have about a news story you read.
- Write a paragraph explaining how you are directly or indirectly affected by a news event.
- List three possible causes for an event in the news. Draw a star by the one you think is the major cause.
- After reading an editorial, write what you think the author's purpose was.
- Compare how two different news sources report the same story. Describe in writing how the reports are alike and how they are different.
- Write a letter to the editor or an editorial expressing your viewpoint on an issue.
- Write a summary of a news report. Include the answers to the 5 W's—*who, what, where, when,* and *why*.
- Write a paragraph that gives your views on what makes a story newsworthy.
- Research careers related to news reporting. Choose one and write a help-wanted ad for that job.
- Write three questions on an index card for a partner to answer by investigating current events reports. One question should pertain to a local issue, one to a national issue, and one to an international issue.

Oral Language and Creative Dramatics

- Present a mock television newscast.
- Perform a re-enactment of a news event.
- Tape record a summary of a news story.
- Interview someone to get his or her opinion about an event.
- Dress as a person involved in a news story and tell what happened to you.
- Participate in a group discussion about a current issue.
- Perform a skit that shows the possible effects of a news event.
- Conduct a mock interview with someone in the news.

Art and Design

Design

- Create a mural that summarizes an event.
- Make a collage with words, headlines, and pictures that relate to a news story.
- Draw an editorial cartoon that expresses your opinion.
- Make a map that identifies important sites relating to a news story.
- Create an exhibit, display, or model that explains part of a news story.
- Make a scrapbook of articles, cartoons, and pictures relating to a news topic.
- Draw a graph or chart that shows information related to a news story.
- Create a timeline that details the order of events.
- Retell a news story through a sequence of drawings.
- Design a display of this month's top news events.

Program Management Tips

Try these suggestions to incorporate a current events program into your learning environment.

Supplies

- Set up a resource center with the daily newspaper, magazines, and other sources of news.
- Keep a recycling bin in the learning environment for newspapers. Empty it on a weekly basis.
- Store in a large can several sets of different colored highlighters for students to use when analyzing news stories or editorials for cause and effect, pros and cons, fact and opinion, and problems and solutions.

A Kiosk Display

Finding space to display current events information is sometimes a challenge. A kiosk is an attractive alternative to a bulletin board. To make a kiosk display, stack several equal-size boxes and tape them together. Cover them with colored paper. Label each side with a different heading—*Local, State, National,* and *International.* Have students post news articles or projects under each heading.

Tapping into the Community

Whether your learning environment is in a school or at home, parents in your community may have resources you are unaware of. Prepare a notice informing them of the topics you are teaching and asking for any help they might contribute:

- Ask families to donate current news magazines they have already read.
- Encourage vacationing students to bring back newspapers from the places they visit.

BULLETIN BOARD DISPLAYS

Design

If possible, devote a large bulletin board in your learning environment to current events. The displays suggested below give the students a chance to be actively involved.

Places and Faces

Assign a small group to choose, post, and number five pictures of people and places in the news. Challenge the rest of the class to identify each person or place, and explain what makes each newsworthy.

Dateline (Country's Name)

Post a map of the country in the center of the bulletin board. Have students pin their news stories to the sides with a strip of yarn connecting each to its place of origin. Change the map and title as needed to match your geographic focus.

What Do You Think About . . . ?

In the center of the bulletin board, post articles, pictures, editorials, letters, and cartoons related to a news event. Surround this display with index cards. Have students write their opinions on cards.

Suggestions

More Current Events Bulletin Board Titles

- News You Can Use
- In the News
- News of the Week
- Kids Should Know

- What's Happening?
- Did You Know . . . ?
- Keeping Current
- What's New?

EVALUATING YOUR PROGRAM

Periodic evaluations let you know what works and what needs improvement in your currents events program.

Evaluation

Student Evaluations

Have students answer these questions:

1. What do you like best about studying current events? What do you like least?

2. What is the most important thing you have learned while studying current events?

3. What types of activities do you enjoy doing most? What types do you enjoy least?

4. Do you learn more working alone, with a partner, in a small group, or in a large group?

5. How would you change our program?

Parent Evaluations

Have parents answer these or other questions tailored specifically to your program:

1. What has your child shared with you about our current events program?

2. Since our program began, do you think your child is more aware of events in the news?

3. Do you see areas that that have not been covered that need to be addressed?

4. Are there areas of the program you feel should be changed or omitted? Why?

Teacher Evaluations

Ask yourself these questions:

1. What activities best stimulate learning?

2. What is the single main goal I have for my program? Is it being achieved?

3. What is the weakest area of my current events program? How can I improve it?

A Teacher's Survival Guide

This chapter is a guide for first-time teachers, home educators, parents, and anyone who would like to implement new ideas in a learning program. You will find practical tips and steps for helping you organize and manage your instructional program. The suggestions and activities provide teacher-tested strategies to help you structure your learning environment before the students arrive. Then use the easy-to-implement ideas on planning, discipline, and instruction to maintain an efficiently structured environment once your students are present.

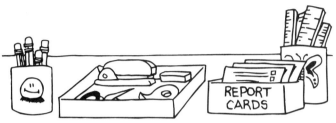

ORGANIZING YOURSELF

Steps to Take

Get off to a great start by spending some time getting organized before school begins. Follow these steps:

1. Gather all the materials you will need—pens, pencils, plan book, skill charts, books, and so on.

2. Plan a rough month-by-month outline of the topics and skills you will be covering. Use the outline as a general guide to help you prepare for the lessons ahead of time. The outline may change as you adapt to the specific needs, interests, and abilities of the class.

3. Write a detailed outline for the first week of school. Include activities that can be inserted or changed at the last minute since schedules and routines may not be firmly established for awhile. Here are some ideas:

   • Storytime—Keep on hand your favorite read-aloud stories or a book of riddles to share with the class.

   • Music—Select three songs to teach students, or choose a taped song to which they may listen and clap out the rhythm.

   • Game—Choose an activity that is simple yet fun. *Example:* Have the students can play "Name Bingo" by making bingo cards with their names.

4. Prepare a "welcome" letter for parents and students. Home educators can compose a "getting started" letter with their children, then use the letter as a springboard for a family discussion.

5. Create a substitute teacher kit. Fill it with a class list, seating chart, floor plan, bus schedule, daily schedule, reproducible activities, special instructions, books to read, emergency procedures, and other items.

Rule of Thumb

A good rule of thumb: Color code your lesson plans. *Example:* Write in red the supplies you need to gather. Write in blue the pages you need to reproduce.

ORGANIZING THE LEARNING ENVIRONMENT

Steps to Take

Get ready for the new school year by planning your classroom carefully. Here are a few steps you can take to get and stay organized:

1. Decide on a decor for your learning environment. Make sure it is active and motivational—one that enhances and enlivens learning—such as a science, social studies, or seasonal themes.

2. Evaluate the physical space in your classroom and organize furniture and other items to use the space most efficiently. Look for potential trouble spots, such as places where some students will not see well or where some might be especially distracted.

3. Create a pocket folder or a big envelope for each month. Store seasonal ideas, pictures, and other items you plan to use during a particular month in its special folder.

4. Label a folder for each day of the week. Then file worksheets and other materials you plan to use that week in the appropriate folders. Reuse these folders week after week.

5. Compile a list of your children's names, addresses, and phone numbers and make several copies. Keep one copy inside your plan book, one copy at home, and another copy at your work area.

6. Set up a work area for adult and student helpers. Be sure to include supplies and a "To Do" list.

7. Set up folders for instructional materials by topic or skill. Use boxes for extensive subjects or units.

   Example: Collect and store in a box all materials for a unit on rain forests—books, worksheets, bulletin board ideas, pictures, magazine articles, art ideas, and so on. Keep adding to the box as you come across more items.

   Store the folders and boxes in a convenient place in your room.

GETTING THROUGH THE FIRST DAY

On the first day of instruction, it is crucial that you establish a consistent pattern of behavior for yourself and for your students. Make certain to also set in place a consistent pattern of how the learning environment will operate on a day-to-day basis. Knowing what to expect helps the students feel comfortable and enables them to begin each day on a clear, positive note.

Note: The checklist that follows is geared to traditional classroom teachers, who usually have the largest number of students to organize and manage. If your learning environment is not a traditional one, simply adapt the checklist to meet your needs.

First Day Checklist

• Be in the learning environment well before the students are expected to arrive.

• Prepare materials for the day, such as name tags, sharpened pencils, and activity sheets.

• Write on the chalkboard a schedule for the day. Both you and the students can refer to the schedule as the day progresses.

• Greet your new students confidently. Smile, introduce yourself, and tell the students exactly where and how to proceed. This establishes an orderly environment.

- Point out to the students where their belongings should be stored and address any matters that need immediate attention.
- Invite the students to introduce themselves to you and their classmates. Discuss the plan/schedule for the day. Talk about what they will be doing and when.

- Show the students where materials and supplies are kept in the room. Then take them on a tour of the school.
- Discuss rules and procedures and invite students to add their input. Explain that the classroom belongs to each of them and that everyone is responsible for making it a pleasant and productive learning environment.
- Choose lessons for the first day that can be done with the whole class. Group learning games are especially motivating and reveal much about individual students. (See First Day Activities below for suggestions.) Make sure each child has some work to take home that day to share with the family.
- Near the end of the day, review with your students what they have accomplished and discuss what to expect tomorrow.
- Send home a welcome letter to parents.

Rule of Thumb

A good rule of thumb: Be very careful throughout the day to maintain an atmosphere in which the students are comfortable, but in which you are in control. Your words and actions will set the tone. If you are consistently firm, fair, and kind, your students will respect you and enjoy learning.

First Day Activities

Try one or more of these activities the first day of class.

Suggestions

Super Six—Begin this (and every) morning by having the class do the "Super Six." These are problems that the class solves while you take roll, collect lunch money, or do other routine tasks. The problems may vary from math questions to riddles to geography trivia. Children who do not finish may work on the problems during the day.

Book Talk—Share a favorite book with your class and read all or part of it aloud. Explain why the book is one of your favorites. Then let your students share their reactions to what you read. Later, have them talk about their favorite books with the class.

Artists at Work—Introduce a short art lesson. Here are two easy ideas:

- **What Is It?**—Draw an interesting line on the chalkboard and have the students copy it on sheets of paper. Encourage every child to create a drawing with that line.
- **Patterns Challenge**—Have each student fold a sheet of drawing paper into eighths and then unfold the paper. Instruct the class to use lines, colors, and shapes to make a different pattern in each of the sections.

PLANNING YOUR LESSONS

Planning

With each successful lesson or project you complete, your self-assurance as an instructor grows. The key to success is thorough planning. Writing lesson plans is one routine that helps you plan specific goals for the class and at the same time encourages you to think about how you can achieve those goals.

A lesson plan usually states one or more objectives, a list of materials needed, the procedure to use, and a means for evaluating the lesson. *Tip:* Make objectives specific and observable. You should be able to tell after the lesson whether or not the objective was met. *Example:* The children will identify parts of a flowering plant.

Your local school district may have books and curriculum guides that are useful when planning the lesson. These materials may offer suggestions for units of study and sample lesson plans.

Tips for Planning Lessons

Most elementary school teachers must plan a variety of lessons each day. Here are some tips to help you plan your lessons efficiently and maintain a positive, realistic attitude about your workload.

- **Plan out your week.** A grid with the days written at the top and the subjects at the left will help you organize your lessons and keep track of what goals you want to reach. For example:

	Monday	Tuesday	Wednesday	Thursday	Friday
Math	Classify geometric shapes	Cut out pictures of shapes	Make patterns	Investigate properties of 3-d shapes	Build with 3-d shapes

- **Share ideas with other teachers.** *Examples:* one teacher may have suggestions for setting up a social studies center; another may have ideas for teaching art.

- **Every so often trade classes with other teachers in your school.** Teachers have different strengths and interests. A teacher who loves physical education may enjoy teaching it to your class in return for your taking her class for music.

- **Pace yourself.** Focus on gathering ideas and materials one subject at a time. For example, devote one month to collecting ideas for hands-on science activities and schedule the next month for finding ways to increase students' writing skills.

- **Keep your lesson plan book.** It will save you time when you are planning next year's lessons, especially if you have included a record of the library books, films, and other materials you have used.

HELPING YOUR STUDENTS GET ORGANIZED

Require students to take a share of the responsibility for the day-to-day operation of the class. Here are a few ways to get your students involved:

- Make a jobs list for the class. Assign one job to a student each week, and write his/her name on the appropriate place on the list.

- Set aside a regular time for group clean-up.

- Designate one or more baskets in your work area for children to place notes from home, lunch money, book orders, and other items.

- Set up a central supply area where students can go independently to get materials such as paper, pencils, and scissors. Assign a student to monitor the supply area.

- Establish a special place where lists, messages, and important announcements are posted. Help each student get in the habit of checking the postings daily for information.

- Supply each student with a large envelope to be used as a "briefcase" for carrying homework and other papers to and from school.

- Encourage students to bring shoe boxes to keep in their desks for small items.

- Assign a student helper to gather and organize assignments for an absent child. The helper can then act as "student teacher" for the child when he/she returns.

- Establish routines with your class. For example, if you have independent reading time immediately after lunch, students should know they are to come into the classroom after the lunch period and begin reading on their own.

Rule of Thumb

A good rule of thumb: Let students create a color-coded personal portfolio for each subject area. These can be made from manila folders or from 11" x 17" (279 x 432 mm) sheets of heavy construction paper. Manila folders can be color coded by marking the tabs. Construction paper portfolios can be given a designated color for each subject. For example, a red folder can be used for storing math-related work such as assignments, contracts, and homework. *Tip:* Every so often, set aside a time to clean out the files.

It's in the Numbers!

Here is a sure-fire technique to organize students quickly! Give each student a "PIN" number like those used by banks. Assign 1 to the first student on your class list, 2 to the second student, and so on. Tell students that their special numbers belongs only to them and that they will use the numbers all year long. Post the numbers and the students' names near your work area for easy reference.

Suggestions

Below are a few ways PIN numbers can be used. You are sure to think of many more as the year progresses.

- Ask students to write their PIN numbers on the upper-right corner of every assignment they turn in. Then collect the papers in numerical order for easy grade recording.

- Use PIN numbers for an orderly way to line up or divide for games. This eliminates the struggle for line position, and you can even reinforce skills by calling numbers according to attributes. *Example:* Instruct students with even PIN numbers to line up on the left.

- Print each student's PIN number on a wooden stick and place all the sticks in a can. When you want to choose a student to answer a question or do a task, draw a stick. Leave "used" sticks out until everyone has been called.

MOTIVATING YOUR STUDENTS

Steps to Take

You can set up your learning environment, teaching units, and reward system to motivate your students. Here are some helpful tips:

- Establish an atmosphere of ownership, community, and shared responsibility in your learning environment. Refer to things as "ours"—our work area, our materials, etc.

- Explain to students that it is their job to learn and prepare themselves for the next level. You are there to help them.

- Let your students know that you accept, care about, and believe in them. Do not just think it, say it!

- Do things *with* your students. Teacher participation is a real motivator for students! For example, if your students are playing a group game, be one of the participants. When your class is painting, paint your own picture, too.

- Give your students opportunities to make decisions about some aspects of their learning.

- Balance your instructional program to include individual, partner, small-group, and whole-group instruction.

- Encourage students to work together cooperatively and to offer help to one another.

- Vary your teaching methods—lecture, discussion, experimentation, hands-on activities, and so on. Help your students understand why a particular lesson has value to them.

- Keep parents informed and involved as much as possible. Invite them to take active roles in their children's learning.

- Hold mini-conferences with your students to discuss their progress.

- Develop a fair reward system for excellent effort, work, and behavior.

MANAGING DISCIPLINE

Getting into Focus

Maintaining order is a priority each learning day. But just as there is no one solution for every problem, there is no perfect discipline management system. It is up to you to give students clear expectations for behavior and conduct by establishing rules that govern your learning environment. Here are a few basics with which to begin:

1. Kindness counts. Be fair and respect others.

2. Keep hands, feet, and objects to yourself.

3. Speak at appropriate times. Share your thoughts during discussions or group work. Keep quiet while others are speaking, while lining up, and while directions are being given.

4. Listen carefully. Give the person who is speaking your full attention. Follow directions.

5. Work to your best ability. Complete your work as best as you can and as independently as possible.

80

A Discipline Strategy

Communication

It can be difficult to be consistent with your discipline policy day after day. To run an effective program, however, you must not let changing circumstances or your own moods tempt you to relax your standards. When you see a behavior problem, you need a step-by-step approach like the one below to get a student back on track.

1. **Verbal warning**—rule reminder

2. **Time out**—removal from the scene or from others

3. **Withdrawal of a privilege**—recess, break, or activity (Follow up with a private conference with the student.)

4. **Note or call home**—involve parent (Home educators can hold a family meeting.)

5. **Detention**—always notify parent first

6. **Parent conference**—include student and/or principal

Rule of Thumb

A good rule of thumb: Never get into a debate—avoid giving students opportunities to manipulate you!

MANAGING INSTRUCTION

A sound approach to managing instruction is through flexible grouping. This means that your instructional program includes whole-group, small-group, partner, and individual activities. Choose the type of grouping you feel is best suited to the activity.

Planning

Whole Group (Instructor directed)
All students in the class are treated as a single group. This not only fosters group coherence, but also makes everyone feel included. Activities such as shared reading are appropriate for whole-group instruction.

Small Group (Instructor directed)
Several students are grouped together to focus on one activity. This method is effective for teaching students of similar abilities or for those needing the same skill.

Cooperative Learning Groups (Student directed)
This is also a small group, but the object is to have students with varied abilities work cooperatively to accomplish a learning goal. This fosters communication and the development of social and leadership skills. Problem-solving activities are especially well suited for cooperative learning groups.

Partner or Individual Work (Student directed)
One or two students work on self-directed activities. This is a great technique for research, long-term projects, journals, learning centers, and activities in which students can make discoveries on their own.

Managing Flexible Grouping

Getting into Focus

Your day may include any number of groupings—some taking place concurrently! You have these responsibilities:

- Deciding what skills are to be learned

- Preparing materials, space, and assignment of groups

- Monitoring progress and intervening when necessary

- Offering support and encouragement

- Evaluating the progress of the group activity

Providing for Students Who Finish Work Early

Students work at different speeds. Here are suggestions for keeping early finishers involved and motivated while their classmates are working:

Suggestions

- Each day write on the chalkboard a list of things that students can do after they have handed in their work. For example, you can give students the option of playing a board game, making a bookmark advertising a book, drawing with colored chalk, or listening to a taped story.

- Set up ongoing activities for students to do in their spare time. The following work well any time of year:

Class Riddle Book—Leave writing paper, riddle books, and a three-ringed binder on a table. Tell students to choose riddles they like, copy the questions on the front of the papers, and write the answers on the backs. After making humorous pictures to go with their riddles, they place their papers in the binder for the class to enjoy.

Puzzle Corner—Keep an assortment of mazes, word searches, crossword puzzles, dot-to-dot pictures, math puzzles, and other fun activity pages in a handy place for students. If you wish, let students create their own puzzles for their classmates to try.

Class Theme Chart—Post a sheet of chart paper in the room. Write a title at the top to indicate the theme, and have students glue on appropriate items. *Example:* for a *long e* chart, have students write *long e* words on pieces of paper or cut out magazine pictures (tree, key, and so on) and glue them to the chart. For a color chart, have the class glue on pictures or items of a particular color. During a study of the rain forest, have students make a chart highlighting rain forest animals.

Rule of Thumb

A good rule of thumb: Make sure that during the week all students, not just early finishers, are given a chance to do the "extra" activities described above.

MANAGING PAPERWORK

The learning environment is a mini-business and it generates a lot of paperwork. You have many kinds of records to keep—from daily grades to maintaining yearly permanent records. It can seem overwhelming!

Developing efficient administrative skills is an important objective. Establish a routine for handling paperwork and stick to it! *Tip:* Begin by organizing your work into small, manageable goals. Create folders for various types of tasks. Label the folders and sort them in order of priority. For example, a "Daily to Do"

Suggestions

folder may contain the day's assignments to check, a note to answer, and a list of materials you need to gather for the next day. Daily paperwork will almost always be first priority.

Here is a sampling of other types of paperwork you may be responsible for. Tip for home educators: Be sure to find out in advance the requirements for homeschooling your children.

Planning

Weekly—lesson plans, reports home, contracts, lists

Monthly—parent letters, attendance records, progress reports, supply and requisition order forms

Quarterly—report cards, conferences and notes, portfolio and permanent record updates

Yearly—substitute folder, homework policy, special requests, testing and assessment records

Ongoing—portfolio upkeep, parent contact records, attendance, and of course, checking and grading homework and assignments!

Rule of Thumb

A good rule of thumb: Use codes to fill in missing spaces in your attendance records or grade book. *Example:* use a circle for an absence, then later fill in an *EX* for "excused" or *M* for "missing work." This technique saves you from questioning blanks later. Plus, if you write in pencil, you can change or update a code at any time!

PREPARING REPORT CARDS AND PARENT CONFERENCES

Whatever your educational setting—school or home—keeping good records is essential when it comes time to report progress. The following tips may be helpful:

Evaluation

Do not wait until the end of the year or even a scheduled reporting period to inform parents about behavior, attendance, or academic problems. Let them know your concerns right away through a call or written notice.

It is vital to be able to back up your reports with accurate records. Behavior problems should be noted with anecdotal records that include dates and the specific behaviors observed. Attendance problems should be reflected in records noting absences and late arrivals. Academic problems should be backed up by your grade book and a folder of work samples.

Even if a student is progressing nicely and you have no particular concerns to report, you still need to be able to justify the grades you give. Keep a work folder on every student to use as your own reference when preparing report cards and to share with parents at conferences.

Report Cards

Plan ahead for completing report cards. They usually take more time than you anticipate! Assemble your records and materials at least a week before they are due to go home. *Tip:* Keep report card comments brief but specific. Always begin with a positive comment, even in cases where grades are poor or there are other problems.

Students are often apprehensive about report cards. It is a good idea to tell them about their report cards before they are sent home. Meet with the student for a few minutes to show him the grades he has earned while briefly discussing them.

Conferences

Communication

A parent conference provides the opportunity to focus on an individual student's learning experiences and gives the educator insight into the student's home environment. Academic progress, effort, and behavior are discussed jointly. For home educators, the conference may involve a district supervisor who will evaluate your teaching methods and your child's progress.

Conference Preparation

Suggestions

- Complete report cards.
- Check that each student has a complete work folder.
- Arrange an appointment schedule and chart.
- Schedule and confirm appointments (by telephone or slip).
- Gather textbooks and other sample materials.
- File the report card and any other information you want to share with the parent in each student's folder.
- Arrange the folders in the order of your appointments.

Conference Tips

- Post your conference schedule on the door.
- Greet parents by name. Be sure you are aware if the child's last name is different from the parent's.
- Share the report card and work folder.
- Provide note paper and pens for parents to jot notes.
- Always begin and end with a positive statement.
- Stay on the subject. Keep the conference on track.
- If you are unsure what a parent is trying to communicate, paraphrase and ask if you are correct.
- Let parents who disagree with you express their views. Then schedule another meeting, perhaps with a support person in attendance.
- Tell parents what they can do to help the their child at home.

Kids as Curators–Museum Explorations

Museum exploration is a wonderful way to enrich and extend your students' learning. This chapter offers many practical ideas, tips, and steps for experiencing art, science, natural history, history, and children's museums. There are suggestions and activities to assist you in making the most of your museum excursions. And if there are no museums nearby? You can transform your learning environment into a variety of mini-museums.

MUSEUMS A TO Z

Investigation

There are thousands of museums and museum-like sites in the United States. Most can be classified into three main categories, with many overlapping:

- **Art**—Some art museums feature many periods and styles. Others focus on one type of art, such as folk art, ethnic art, western art, modern art, or photography.

- **Science**—Natural history museums feature plants, animals, and minerals found in nature. Science and technology museums explore math and science concepts. Many people also consider planetariums, nature centers, zoos, aquariums, and botanical gardens as science museums.

- **History**—History museums show artifacts or events of the past. Some are comprised of historic buildings. Others focus on a specific theme, such as the Holocaust or transportation. Living history museums re-enact life in an earlier period.

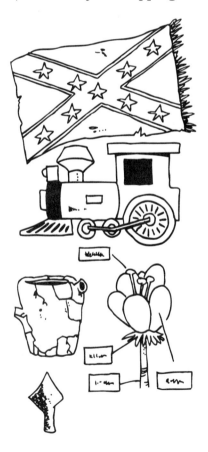

TIPS FOR MUSEUM FIELD TRIPS

Steps to Take

These tips can help make a museum field trip a rewarding educational experience:

1. **Contact the museum's education office.** Ask if guided tours are available and if there is a choice of programs. Check to see if there are materials you can preview and use on your field trip. Find out costs, age requirements, and suggested length of visits.

2. **Visit the museum without students.** Learn what the museum offers that applies to your studies.

3. **Attend teacher workshops if possible.** Many museums have workshops for educators that give additional background information about the exhibits.

4. **Choose a focus for your field trip.** Some museums are too large to be explored in a two-hour trip.

5. **Enlist the help of parent volunteers—the more the better.** Students exploring in small groups will be able to ask more questions and see the exhibits more easily. Volunteers will enjoy the visit more if they are guiding fewer students. Let parents know what your goals are for the visit and what their responsibilities are.

6. **Give students time for both directed and undirected explorations.** You may want to allot three-quarters of the field trip to tours or directed activities (scavenger hunt, exhibit analysis, planned sketching) and the rest of the time to supervised free exploration.

Writing

7. **Write thank-you notes.** Give students real-life writing experiences by having them write thank-you notes to the museum staff mentioning facts they learned or things they especially enjoyed.

Rule of Thumb

A good rule of thumb: If you have a large group, you may want students to wear some sort of instantly identifiable item, such as a school T-shirt, to help keep track of them. A set of white painter's caps labeled with your school's name—*Liberty School Student Investigator*— might also work for the preteen age group.

What if There Is No Museum Close by . . .

Suggestions

Perhaps the nearest museum is too far away from your learning environment to make visiting a practical option. Your students can still have museum experiences!

- **Ask if the museum has an outreach program.** Many large museums have resources they can bring to your community.

- **Turn your learning environment into a museum.** The following section tells how.

CREATING YOUR OWN MINI-MUSEUM

Suggestions

Invite your children to create their own "museum" to supplement or substitute for a visit to a museum. (For simplicity, the suggestions are worded to address traditional classrooms. If your learning environment differs, simply adapt the suggestion to your situation.)

Museum Space

Your museum can take a variety of forms depending on the number of people involved and the size of exhibits.

- **Classroom Corner**—A corner of the room is set aside as the mini-museum. Exhibits are planned and created by groups and changed each month.

- **Classroom**—Everyone contributes to turning the entire room—tables, counters, walls, and bulletin boards—into a showcase of art, science, or history.

- **Large Room**—The cafeteria, multipurpose room, or other large central space is used by one class, by all classes in a single grade, or by the whole school to create a large museum.

- **Outdoors**—A living history museum is created outside on the playground, field, or blacktop.

Display Ideas

Design

A few decorating ideas can spruce up your museum.

- **Tables**—Cover tables with white or solid-colored cloth sheets or paper.
- **Display pedestals**—Gather boxes of all sizes. Cover them with colored butcher paper. Several can be stacked together to make kiosks.
- **Frames**—Post all artwork on large sheets of black paper. The black background will allow viewers to focus on the art.
- **Display signs**—Select a uniform style, such as large index cards mounted on colored construction paper.

Who Works in a Museum?

Museums employ a variety of workers. Here are some positions you may consider for your class museum:

- **Director**—Oversees the entire museum.
- **Curators**—Locate, choose, and plan the contents and exhibits of the museum.
- **Graphic Designers**—Create signs, posters, and labels for the exhibits.
- **Conservators**—Repair displays that are damaged.
- **Registrar**—Keeps a catalog of each item in the museum's collection.
- **Crew**—Sets up and moves displays.
- **Publicity Director**—Informs the public about events and programs at the museum.
- **Docents (Volunteers)**—Conduct tours of the museum.

Investigation

Who Will Visit Your Museum?

Choose your audience when the museum is in the planning stages.

- **Another class in the same grade**—Share your work with another class that is studying the same topics.
- **A younger class**—Pair up your students with younger buddies, and guide them around the museum to introduce them to "big kid" topics.
- **The entire school**—Invite classes of all grades to tour your museum.
- **Families**—Set up a special museum program during school or in the evening so parents and families can share in your learning.

Suggestions

VISITING AN ART MUSEUM

Have students bring a pencil and a notebook, sketchbook, or clipboard to the art museum.

Focus on Elements of Art

Choose an element of art to discuss before your trip. Then have students look for examples of it in many works of art. Direct students to select three pieces of art and describe in detail how the element relates to them.

- **Color**—One color, multicolored, bright colors, subdued colors, realistic colors, dominant color
- **Line**—Thick, thin, straight, curved, jagged, bold, delicate, patterned
- **Texture**—Rough, smooth, ridged, shiny, dull
- **Shape**—Realistic, distorted, geometric
- **Space**—Balanced, off-balance, full, empty, near, distant

Investigation

Focus on Artists

1. Have students make two lists during their visit:

   - Artists of whom they have heard or studied.

   - Artists new to them whose work they like. (Beside one artist's name, students can briefly describe a work of art and why they like it.)

2. Have students look for two works of art they like by the same artist and describe how the works are similar and how they are different.

Writing

Focus on Period or Culture

Choose two periods of time or two cultures and have students compare and contrast the artwork. *Examples:* Northwest Coastal Indians and Northeast Woodland Indians; medieval paintings and Renaissance paintings.

CREATING YOUR OWN ART MUSEUM
Famous Artists and Their Masterpieces

Suggestions

Gather a collection of art books and biographies of artists. Have each student choose an artist and research the artist's life and works. Direct students to select one of their artist's better-known paintings or sculptures and create a reproduction of it. Display the works on walls or tables around your classroom or in your museum corner.

Have students create brief signs for their displays giving background information about the pieces or interesting facts about the artists. Or have students dress as and pretend to be their chosen artists and explain the displays to the class or other museum visitors.

Impressionists' Gallery

Choose a period or style of art you want students to study, such as impressionism, cubism, or surrealism. After reading about it and looking at examples, guide students in creating original artwork in that style. Display their works in your museum. If possible, intersperse reproductions of artists' works of that same period or style.

·MONET·

End-of-Year Museum

Create a museum at the end of the year featuring students' artwork. Group the works by period, region, or style—Greek vases, medieval stained glass, African masks, Inuit soap carvings, American quilts, self-portraits, mobiles. Have students write paragraphs about themselves on index cards labeled "About the Artist." Let students post the cards beside their favorite works of art.

VISITING A SCIENCE MUSEUM

Most science and technology museums have hands-on displays that demonstrate science and math concepts. Let students be active explorers in the museum and do follow-up writing in the classroom.

Rule of Thumb

A good rule of thumb: Have students work with partners when visiting a hands-on museum. Two heads are often better than one for reading directions and thinking about results.

Hands-On Exhibits

Investigation

Before your trip, tell students to look for an exhibit that teaches them something they did not already know. After the trip, have students sketch and describe the exhibit and write the science facts they learned from it.

Follow-Up Frames

Write one of these writing frames on the chalkboard before your trip:

Evaluation

I thought the _____ display was the most interesting

because _____.

One thing I learned that I did not know before was _____

_____.

If I were a curator at this museum, I would add an exhibit about

_____ because _____.

When you return from the museum trip, ask students to copy and complete the frame.

CREATING YOUR OWN SCIENCE MUSEUM

Theme Museum

Suggestions

Choose a theme you are studying, such as ecology, the human body, the ocean, or weather. Brainstorm a list of displays, science demonstrations, art projects, or other activities students could do that relate to the theme.

Weather ideas:
- lightning safety tips
- life-size model of the largest hailstone
- design-your-own-snowflakes art activity
- separating light into the colors of the rainbow
- water cycle demonstration
- cloud chart

Let children work in small groups to plan and create an activity or display for the museum.

Hands-On Science Demonstrations

Have students work with a partner and plan a quick hands-on science activity that students or adults could do again and again. Direct pairs to prepare these parts:

- A sign for their activity that includes a title, a question, directions, and a paragraph explaining the results.

- The materials needed to do the activity.

Arrange desks or tables near the walls so that museum visitors can move easily from one activity to another as they explore and learn science concepts.

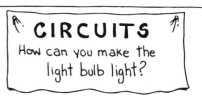

CIRCUITS
How can you make the light bulb light?

VISITING A NATURAL HISTORY MUSEUM

Have students bring paper and a clipboard to the natural history museum.

Animal Scavenger Hunt

Investigation

This idea works well when visiting the animal displays in a natural history museum. Before the trip, brainstorm a list of animal categories such as these:

- herbivore
- carnivore
- omnivore
- bird
- reptile
- mammal
- fish

- desert animal
- forest animal
- endangered or extinct animal
- egg-laying animal
- poisonous animal
- camouflaged animal
- amphibian

Have students draw lines to divide blank sheets of paper into eighths. Let students choose their own eight categories and write each one in a separate box. At the museum, direct them to find and write the name of an animal for each category. On the back of the paper, have each student sketch his/her favorite animal.

Museum ABC's

Direct students to write the alphabet vertically on a sheet of paper. As they journey through the museum, have students try to find one object or animal that begins with each letter and record it on their papers. Compare the lists when you return to the classroom.

Writing

Animal, Vegetable, or Mineral?

This activity lets students classify what they see on their visit. Have each student draw three columns on a sheet of paper and label them Animal, Vegetable, and Mineral. Ask students to find and list 10 items for each category.

CREATING YOUR OWN NATURAL HISTORY MUSEUM

Individual Collections

Suggestions

Let students choose something from nature (real or models) they would like to display—shells, rocks, leaves, dinosaurs, seeds, plants, butterflies, and so on. Then ask them to decide if their collection would work better as a poster or as a 3-D display. For displays, have students make stands of various heights by recycling food boxes and containers and covering them with paper.

Miniature Habitats

Make miniature habitat displays using shoe boxes or other small cardboard boxes. First brainstorm a list of habitats—Arctic, Antarctic, tropical rain forest, Sonoran desert, Sahara desert, Australian outback, North American prairie, African savanna, deciduous forest, tundra, ocean, marsh, and so on. Have students work alone, in pairs, or in small groups to plan and create a habitat display:

1. Choose a habitat.
2. Research the habitat to learn about its plants, animals, and typical land formations.
3. Decide how to make your miniature habitat.
   - What will your background drawing show?
   - Of what plants or animals will you make models?
   - Will you make clay, cardboard, or other models?
   - What will your ground surface be?
4. Make the habitat display.
5. Create a sign identifying parts of your habitat.

AFRICAN SAVANNA
1. Giraffe	5. Lion
2. Rhino	6. Grass
3. Water hole	7. Baobab tree
4. Acacia tree	8. Wildebeest

VISITING A HISTORY MUSEUM

Investigation

Here are some history museum activities your students can do that encourage critical thinking.

Then and Now Analysis

Have students divide sheets of paper into two columns labeled "Then" and "Now." As they travel through the museum, have students note and describe objects, activities, or events from the past and compare them with current objects, activities, and events.

Write a Journal

This activity works well for a living history museum or a history museum that details everyday life during a specific time period. Before the trip, tell students that when they return, they will be writing journal entries in which they pretend to be living during the period of history featured at the museum. Suggest that they prepare by taking notes while visiting the exhibits. Post the finished journal entries on a bulletin board.

Writing

History Time Line

Design

This activity is designed for museums that showcase a continuum of time, not just one period in history. Have pairs of students choose a group of people, a category, or an event that is featured at the museum, such as women, toys, or westward expansion. Direct students to take notes detailing how their topic changed through history. Back in the classroom, have each pair create a time line illustrating the information they learned.

CREATING YOUR OWN HISTORY MUSEUM

Suggestions

Everyday Life During . . .

Choose a period of time you are studying, such as the Middle Ages. Divide the class into four groups—home, work, school, and play. Assign each group a different display area, and have them fill it with posters, models, and other displays that teach museum visitors about their category.

A Living History Museum

Choose a topic to research and study intensively, such as the Aztec civilization at its peak or immigrants arriving at Ellis Island. As a class, plan different activities or an event students could re-enact to teach museum visitors about that period of history. Have students sign up for the parts they want to play. Then direct groups to plan and prepare these four main components:

• Costumes

• Props

• Activities they will do

• Lines they will speak

"Wax Museum": Famous People from the Past

Let students pretend to be "wax figures" in their own museum. Have each student research a famous person in history and create a poster with key facts about that person's life written in large print. Next have the students plan and create costumes. Arrange your wax figures chronologically in a large area, with their posters displayed on the wall beside them. Tell your students to stand as still as possible. Let museum visitors walk by and read about the famous people. Remind visitors that they may not touch the wax figures.

VISITING A CHILDREN'S MUSEUM

The focus of children's museums is "hands-on" learning. Some museums are devoted entirely to children. Others have special sections that appeal to younger visitors. Large museums often have exhibits created especially for different age groups (children up to 12 years old).

Museum Tips

Suggestions

• Encourage students to read the signs. Many displays provide detailed information that older students can read and understand.

• Direct students to ask themselves "What did I learn?" when finishing one exhibit and moving to another.

• Guide students to appropriate exhibits, especially if they become "glued" to an area designed for much younger children.

Steps to Take

How Is a Children's Museum Run?

Coordinate your visit so the director or a member of the staff can show your children how the museum operates.

Before the Field Trip . . .

Prepare a few weeks in advance by eliciting questions from students. Send them to the museum. You may also want to request that your tour guide explain ways staff members use math, reading, or writing in their jobs.

During the Field Trip . . .

Allow time for students to explore the museum exhibits before going on a guided tour. This will make it easier for them to concentrate once they are behind the scenes.

After the Field Trip . . .

Have students work in small groups to brainstorm ideas for new exhibits. Ask each group to write a thank-you note to your tour guide and include a sketch and description of their favorite new exhibit idea.

CREATING YOUR OWN CHILDREN'S MUSEUM

Career Displays

Make a career exhibit. Have each student choose an occupation and research it. Direct students to gather props or create displays for their chosen careers. List all the careers on the chalkboard. Have students think of different ways to classify them—outdoor jobs, service jobs, retail businesses, jobs in the arts, and so on. Select a few general headings that everyone agrees on and group the career displays in your museum accordingly.

Suggestions

Traveling Around the U.S.A.

Divide your class into groups that correspond to these regions of the country—New England, Middle Atlantic, Southeast, Midwest, Rocky Mountain, Southwest, and Pacific Coast. Have each group create a display that informs students about that region and includes activities for them to do.

Learning About Literature

Make a museum exhibit that teaches younger students about stories and books. As a class, choose some general categories and come up with subtopics—elements of a story (characters, setting, plot, theme); parts of a nonfiction book (title page, copyright page, table of contents, body, glossary, index); types of books (fiction, non-fiction, folklore, poetry, picture books, fantasy, science fiction). Have students sign up for a category, then work as a group to create a hands-on display about it. Invite younger classes to tour your finished exhibit.

Using Community Resources

Although communities may vary, they have many resources in common. This chapter contains ideas for finding and using the people and places in your community to the fullest advantage. There are suggestions for designing curriculum activities that are educational and fun as well as ideas for using the resources in your community as springboards to practical and well-rounded educational experiences for your students.

GETTING STARTED

Investigation

You know that you want your learning environment to reach beyond the walls of your classroom. But how do you find out about the people and places that may be valuable resources in your community? Here are some ways:

- Your *community newspaper* is a good place to start in finding local resources—people and places of interest right in your own backyard. Hometown newspapers often profile community members who have interesting hobbies or occupations. Through the newspaper, you may be able to invite a local children's author, an animal collector, or a world traveler to visit your classroom. Another way to find an expert in just about any field is to use the *Yellow Pages* telephone directory.

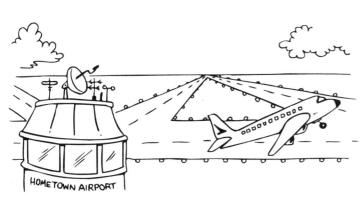

- A trip to the nearest *library* is a good next step. Ask the reference librarian for directories or brochures on places of local interest, especially for children. You may find that a local author has compiled a directory of interesting places to visit with children. The library also has national directories of museums and historical societies that will help you locate the ones nearest you.

- Call or write your local *transit district* and inquire about a guide to interesting places that are serviced by the bus or train routes.

• The *Chamber of Commerce* may also have information that will be useful to you. Personnel can tell you about local organizations, businesses, and industries. You may be surprised to find that many businesses, large and small, will open their doors to you. A telephone call to a local manufacturer will tell you if tours are available. Perhaps you and your students can visit a large automotive assembly line or a small glass-blowing operation. You might discover that a local leather goods manufacturer will give your students a tour and allow them to make small leather items themselves. Or, a local catering service may give tours that include a hands-on experience in preparing a food item.

Rule of Thumb

A *good rule of thumb:* Even though the days and hours of operation for public places are listed in the printed material you find, it is always a good idea to phone ahead. The size of your group may require special reservations, buildings may be undergoing renovations, or the hours may change with the seasons.

RESOURCE PEOPLE IN THE CLASSROOM

Invite resource people into your classroom and you are certain to create excitement and give students memorable experiences. According to one education expert, the benefits of bringing in a resource person far outweigh the efforts that go into planning and organizing it.

Ideas

Police and fire department personnel are obvious choices for a valuable program that appeals to many age levels. Not only are they available in almost every community, they are usually very willing and happy to visit.

Consider inviting senior citizens to your classroom. This is a great way to tap into a vast source of information and experience. Seniors may have firsthand knowledge about a particular time in recent history that the class is studying. Or, they may be able to talk about how your community has changed and developed over the years.

Invite students' parents to share hobbies or occupations with your group. Home educators, too, can ask other parents or neighbors to speak about their specialties.

Do not overlook historical societies! They can provide speakers who may bring visual aids, such as dolls dressed in colonial garb, household items from another era, or a slide presentation of your neighborhood over the years.

Rule of Thumb

A *good rule of thumb:* Be sure to take time before the day of the presentation to meet and/or talk with resource people who will be visiting your learning environment. Tell the guests a little about your group—its size and age level—so they can be prepared, particularly if your students are very young.

Also give your students some background on your guest. List on chart paper the questions students want to ask. You may also want to assign who will ask them, so none of the questions are forgotten.

DIGGING FOR RESOURCES

Suggestions

Once you start digging, you are sure to find a wealth of resources in your community that can provide valuable learning experiences for students. Here is an annotated list of places you may want to consider:

- **Airport.** Watch planes take off and land. See how baggage and ticketing are handled. Some airports give tours that include repair shops, hangars, and cockpits.

- **Bookstore.** There may be a children's bookstore near you. Ask for a tour that shows students how the store is operated. Then stay for story time and craft time.

- **Farmers' Market.** View the array of locally grown produce and select some to purchase and take home.

- **Guide Dog School.** Students can learn how dogs are fed and cared for at the training facility and about the special training needed to guide people who are sightless.

- **International or Ethnic Center.** Centers devoted to one or more cultural/ethnic groups sponsor arts programs, displays, and festivals. Call for a calendar of events.

- **College Campus.** A visit to a college campus is exciting for elementary students. Someday they may be students there! Some colleges give tours of classrooms, athletic facilities, theaters, planetariums, science labs, and so on.

- **Libraries.** Take advantage of the many special services offered by local libraries, such as story hours, reading clubs, special collections, and displays. In addition, some libraries are dedicated to the lives and works of prominent people—for example, presidential libraries. Look in your local library for the names of other regional libraries (libraries belonging to industry, companies, associations, clubs, foundations, institutes, and societies.)

- **Dance Studio.** Observe a class or a rehearsal. Afterward, talk to the dancers to find out how long they have been studying, how often they practice, and how many classes they take. Learn what a choreographer does.

- **Historical Museum/Historical Society.** Make history come alive with tours of historical buildings, folk art demonstrations, docents in period dress who speak in period dialect, and interactive exhibits of all kinds. Some museums offer traveling exhibits, special interest clubs, school loan services, and teacher training and assistance. (*The Official Museum Directory* published by R. R. Bowker lists U.S. museums by state.)

- **Ecological Center.** Take a guided nature walk. Be sure to bring your sunblock, hat, water, snack, and binoculars!

- **Opera Company or Symphony Orchestra.** These types of organizations educate the next generation of audiences by bringing professional quality programs to the schools. In addition, a symphony orchestra may present a series of special youth concerts in its facility. Many opera companies have educational outreach programs that bring small productions of original operas, written especially for today's students, right to your school. They provide teacher's guides and sponsor workshops for teachers and students.

Ideas

As you explore your community's resources, you will discover many other possibilities. Here are some of them.

- Animal Shelter
- Anthropology Museum
- Armed Forces Reserve Center
- Art Museum
- Arboretum
- Artist's Studio
- Bakery
- Bagel Shop
- Braille Institute
- Car Wash
- Cable Company
- Cider Mill/Apple Farm
- Civic Center
- Court
- Dairy
- Duck Pond
- Environmental Agency
- Ecological Reserve
- Farm
- Fire Department
- Ferry Ride
- Fine Arts Center
- Florist
- Grocery Store
- Hobby Shop

- Ice Cream Store
- Lighthouse
- Magic Shop
- Maritime Museum
- Marsh
- Military Base
- Nature Center
- Newspaper
- Nursery
- Observatory
- Optometrist
- Park
- Pet Grooming Shop
- Performing Arts Center
- Planetarium
- Police Department
- Postal Service
- Radio Station
- Railroad Station
- Recycling Center
- Stables
- Stadium
- Travel Agency
- Water Treatment Plant
- Zoo

Rule of Thumb

*A **good rule of thumb:*** If you are planning a trip to a grocery store, bagel shop, plant nursery, or other retail establishment, always make arrangements in advance with the store manager or shop owner to make sure your group can be accommodated.

PLANNING A LEARNING EXPERIENCE

Choosing a Resource

Teachers generally select a community resource that matches the established curriculum for their particular grades. If you are planning an outing for a preschool play group or a homeschool group, be sure to consider what is most age-appropriate for your children. Television stations, radio stations, and newspapers generally are happy to provide tours for older students (but they may limit the size of the group). A preschool group can benefit from a carefully supervised trip to the duck pond (with a supply of crumbs to feed the ducks), or a trip to a nursery at holiday time to see different kinds of evergreen trees. Teachers can get together with other teachers to pool their knowledge and ideas for using community people and resources. Ask the school media specialist or librarian to compile a directory. Survey the teachers in your school and publish the information. Why not make it a district-wide project?

Steps to Take

Parents and home educators can pool their resources, too. It is a good idea for parents who are teaching children at home to get together with other homeschooling parents for field trips. This gives parents a chance to support each other's efforts, and gives the students the benefit of social exchange with other students.

Things to Do Before You Go

Investigation

Involve your students right from the start. Give them an opportunity to choose between two places you have selected. Take a classroom vote to decide.

If your class is visiting a public facility, such as a museum, have them compose a letter requesting a visitor's brochure or other information. *Tip:* It is best to limit this to one letter per class.

Get out your collection of local maps (travel bureaus, local Chambers of Commerce, etc., have free maps) and have the students work in groups to study them. Instruct each group of students to locate their school and their destination, and then plan a route. Have each group explain the route they chose and tell why they chose it.

Enlist the help of your school librarian in selecting nonfiction books (such as information books and biographies related to the trip) for the students to read beforehand. Do not forget to ask for fiction and poetry, too!

Adults sometimes read a good novel that is set in their vacation destination to enhance their enjoyment of the trip. Good children's books of different genres can do the same for your students. Before taking a tour of the Postal Service, for example, students will enjoy picture books such as *Stringbean's Trip to the Shining Sea* by Vera Williams (Greenwillow Books) or *Toddle Creek Post Office* by Uri Shulevitz (Farrar, Straus and Giroux). Books such as *Linnea in Monet's Garden* by Christina Bjork (R & S Books) and *Miss Rumphius* by Barbara Cooney (Viking Press) are ideal for a trip to a botanical garden or plant nursery. (*Linnea in Monet's Garden* is good for an art museum excursion, as well.) Your librarian can find many more books suited to your grade level.

Rule of Thumb

A good rule of thumb: Have the students prepare several questions in advance to ask of tour guides, managers, workers, or others they will encounter on their visit. Students can report back to the class with the answers when they return.

Use student-made journals or notebooks for sketching interesting things (a skunk, a water lily painting, a dough machine), recording comments (dates, facts, statistics), writing thoughts (this was my favorite part of the marsh because . . .), and even keeping tallies of things that were seen (five kinds of butterflies, four mummies).

Students can use plain newsprint and a black crayon to make rubbings of historical markers, cornerstones, and interesting gravestones. To make the rubbing, have the student place the paper over the object and keep it steady as he rubs with the side of the crayon until the image appears.

Have each student make a "viewer" for focusing on something special. A viewer can be a simple rectangular cardboard frame hung around the neck with a piece of yarn. Outdoors, students can look through the viewers and focus their attention on particular flowers or birds. Indoors, viewers can help them see one part of a painting or sculpture.

Take along a disposable camera (27 exposures) and allow each student to take one snapshot of something for a class album.

Bring a small tape recorder and allow students to take turns recording some of the sounds of their visit.

Things to Do After Your Return

Give your students an opportunity to cap their learning experience with a culminating project, using a medium of their choosing. Provide them with a list of ideas. Here are some examples:

• Use your journal notes and sketches and expand them into a report.

• Make a 3-D model of something from your trip.

• Write captions for the class picture album of the trip.

• Make a display of something you learned on the trip.

• Give a dramatic presentation about something you learned.

• Write a poem about some part of the trip and recite it, using the sounds you tape recorded as a background.

• Make and perform a dance about some part of the trip, using the tape-recorded sounds as a background.

• Make a graph of data gathered on your trip.

- Design and write a brochure about the place you visited.
- Design a poster about the place you visited.
- Write a letter to your parents explaining why you took the trip, what you saw, and what you learned.

Making It Work for You

You can adopt any of the previous ideas that suit your group and the community resource you are using. In the pages that follow are three field trip experiences and specific activities that go with them.

LANGUAGE ARTS: SPORTS STADIUM TOUR

Suggestions

A number of professional sports stadiums give tours, some of them on a daily basis. A phone call to your local or regional stadium can answer your questions about group rates and times, and you can request a packet of information as well. A typical stadium tour may include football and baseball press boxes, luxury boxes, a locker room, a dugout and bullpen, and the dirt track around the field, called the warning track. Students will learn lots of history and trivia about the stadium and the teams.

Sports Journals

Writing

Before your trip, have students construct their own personalized journals. They can make sturdy covers by trimming manila folders with scissors and stapling writing paper inside. Have them decorate the covers with sports logos, equipment, their favorite players, and anything else they like. This notebook can serve many functions.

- Before the trip, have students write about a sports experience they had, whether it was attending a game, playing a sport, or watching a family member play.

- Students can write what they would like to learn, things to observe, and questions they have about the teams and the stadium.

- Have students make a graphic organizer for information they hope to gather. Instruct your students to divide a page of their notebooks into three columns with the headings "Questions," "Answers," and "Details." Have each student fill in the first column before the trip, and the other columns during and after it.

- Instruct students to make notes about their impressions, feelings, and reactions to what they see and hear during the trip.

Ideas

Words and Ideas

Have students brainstorm some words or subjects that they associate with the sports stadium. Make a class list on chart paper. Then have students work in pairs to put the words into categories of their own creation. Instruct them to write factual sentences based on their categorization. After their visit to the stadium, have the students look back at their sentences and correct any misinformation, or add information they have learned.

Project Time

On their return, have each student select a project from a list of language arts assignments like the one below.

- Pretend you are writing from the stadium press box. Describe the highlights of a game you watched.

- Imagine that when you stepped on the field, the stadium was full, you were in uniform, and the crowd cheered. What happened next?

- Find out the history of the word "stadium."

- Make a list of words related to your trip. Write each one on a small card and arrange them in categories: nouns, verbs, and adjectives.

- Choose a sports-related picture book to read aloud. Practice your selection, then share it with a younger child.

- Research the history of the stadium to find out what other events have been hosted there. Make a list of your findings.

SCIENCE: NATURE CENTER TRIP

A visit to a Nature Center is another adventure that is appealing to students of all ages. These centers feature local plants and animals and offer students an opportunity to study habitats. Depending on the type you visit, a Nature Center may have self-guided tours, guided tours, and discovery centers where lectures, demonstrations, and hands-on activities are offered.

Rule of Thumb

A good rule of thumb: Make sure students know they are to leave natural surroundings just as they found them. Explain that they should take nothing with them when they leave, and leave nothing behind.

Collecting Data

On a trip like this, each student should have a scientist's notebook. Have the students make theirs from a manila folder and writing or drawing paper (see "Sports Journals" on page 101). Scientists' notebooks are useful for recording data and information. Here are some specific examples:

- Draw an animal home (habitat) you see.

- Sketch a plant in its habitat.

- Make a color tally of the flowers you see—how many different kinds of blossoms are red, blue, yellow, etc.?

- Write the date, the time, and your observation of something that changed—a fish splashed in the pond, the wind blew leaves off a tree, a bird flew from one branch to another.
- List all the animals you see.
- Choose a spot that is about 2-feet (61-cm) square. List everything that exists in that mini-environment (dirt, grass, insects, air).

A Listening Place

Suggestions

In their excitement over being in a stimulating new environment, your students will probably be talkative and exuberant. That is fine, but remind them that there are things to be learned using only their sense of hearing! Have them find a place to sit for two or three minutes just to listen. Explain that there should be absolutely no talking for this brief period, and that they should listen carefully in order to identify all the sounds they hear. When the exercise is over, discuss what was heard. Were the sounds created by nature or by humans? What sounds did they like? How are sounds important to some animals? Back in the learning environment, have students recall the different sounds they heard while in the Nature Center and list them in two columns: "Nature Sounds" and "People Sounds."

Books for Nature Study

Picture book author and illustrator Jim Arnosky is an observer of nature. His simple, colorful books inspire young naturalists to look at nature with a sharp eye. Before your outing, share with your students his three "Reading Rainbow" books: *Deer at the Brook; Come Out, Muskrats;* and *Raccoons and Ripe Corn* (Lothrop, Lee & Shepard). Have your students take note of the concise descriptions and detailed illustrations that show what a careful observer Arnosky is. Encourage them to be observers, too. When you return from the field trip, have each student write and illustrate something he or she observed, then compile these observations into a book for your classroom library.

SOCIAL STUDIES: BOOKSTORE ADVENTURE

Suggestions

Many of today's bookstores are lively literary places where lots of things are happening! Your students will enjoy learning how a bookstore operates. You may be able to choose from a variety of bookstores in your area—children's bookstores, small independently owned stores, or large chain stores. Some chain stores have a community relations coordinator who can help you with arrangements. Students can find out how a bookstore is run by touring the sales floor and back room. Afterward, there might be an opportunity for young students to hear a storybook read aloud, listen to a storyteller, or make crafts.

Where Do Books Come From?

Before your class visits the bookstore, they can learn how books get to bookstore shelves by reading *How a Book Is Made* by Aliki (T. Y. Crowell). The appealing cartoon format of this book takes the reader from the beginning of a book (how an author gets an idea), through the technical aspects of printing and production, and finally to the bookstore shelves. Students will learn about the people involved in making a book and what they do, including the author, illustrator, editor, publisher, designer, production coordinator, copyeditor, printer, publicist, and salesperson.

Advertising Executives

Invite your students to become advertising executives when they return from their bookstore outing. Have them design a newspaper advertisement for the bookstore you visited. The students should study advertisements to learn some of the important elements. Remind them to use what they know about the store. Suggest that they feature their own favorite book or books in the advertisements.

Promoting Books

Bookstores and other retail establishments sometimes give out small incentive cards to encourage customers to do their shopping there. Every time a book is purchased, a space on the card is punched or initialed. When the card is full, it can be redeemed for credit toward the next purchase. Show your students examples of these cards. Then have students design their own incentive cards. They can use 3" x 5" (76 x 127 mm) index cards and design titles and logos for their cards. Stipulate how many spaces the card must have. Use a special stamp or your initials when a student completes a book. Award a bookmark when the card is full.

Rule of Thumb

A good rule of thumb: No matter what the age or makeup of your learning group, reaching out to your community as part of your instructional program will expand your students horizons and help them gain appreciation for the value of human diversity.

Conducting a Successful Field Trip

Field trips connect your students' learning with the exciting world outside the learning environment. This chapter will help you plan all aspects of the trip, with practical guidelines and tips to help you structure your excursion for optimum organization, management, and active learning. You will also find follow-up activities to enrich your experience and criteria for evaluating the meeting of its educational value.

WHY TAKE A FIELD TRIP?

Planning

The value of taking a field trip is to educate your students through direct experience. By drawing on the community and its resources, your field trip becomes the bridge between the learning environment and the world outside. Field trips increase your students' knowledge about a particular subject, but even more importantly, they may spark students' interest in further exploring a topic. It is vital that the field trip be an extension of your instructional objectives. Keep these things in mind as you establish your trip's goals:

- Determine if a field trip would enhance the learning of a subject or topic in your curriculum. Does the field trip you are considering make a valuable contribution to the larger unit of study on which your students are working?

- Decide on the best time for the excursion. Would the trip be of the most value before introducing the unit, in the middle of it, or at the end? Is the goal of the field trip to expose students to new information or to reinforce learned concepts?

- Develop a lesson plan just as you would for any other lesson. Clearly state the objective. What do you expect your students to learn from this excursion?

- Plan how you can involve your students in the field trip preparations.

Rule of Thumb

A good rule of thumb: Your plans for the field trip must connect your students' experiences to the instructional objective. Make sure your students clearly understand why you are taking them to a particular place and what they are expected to observe, learn, and gain from the experience.

PLANNING YOUR FIELD TRIP

Once you decide that a field trip would be worthwhile, you must plan all aspects of the trip. Careful planning is the key to a successful field trip and entails thoughtful consideration of a multitude of details—some obvious, others less so. Keep these points in mind as you plan your trip:

Steps to Take

1. Contact a knowledgeable representative at the proposed site. Before calling, jot down questions you want to ask. First, tell the representative the size and age level of your group and what you hope to accomplish by the visit. Ask if the site can accommodate your group and what the students can see and do there. Will a guide be provided? Are the tours arranged especially for students? Other things to consider include visitation dates, times, fees, routes, parking, food and drinks, equipment, supplies, and safety rules and regulations. You may also want to inquire about provisions for handicapped children.

2. When you and the representative agree on the details and the date of the visit, check your calendar to determine if the proposed date is in conflict with holidays, test days, and so on. Guard against the possibility of any mix-ups by confirming in writing the day, date, and time of the trip, and any other important details.

3. Plan your transportation to the site. Will you be going by bus or car pool? Confirm these arrangements in writing. If you are transporting students by car, be sure all drivers are properly insured.

4. If the trip is not funded by the school you may need to raise money to cover expenses. You may consider having your students hold a fundraiser to pay for the trip, or you can request funds from parents. If you ask parents to contribute money to fund the trip, make sure you give them a detailed account of how the money will be used.

5. Write a notice to parents well ahead of time informing them of the trip. Include all the details: date, times, transportation plans, funding, objectives, and activities. To ensure they receive this information, ask parents to sign and return a tear-off permission form. If your school does not have a standard permission form, make your own. Include a section for medical emergency information and parent phone numbers.

6. Adequate adult supervision is important for ensuring safety, maintaining control of the group, and assuring a successful learning experience. Invite parents and other responsible adults to help supervise the trip.

7. Once you have the plans in place, begin pre-field trip instructional activities.

Field Trip Etiquette Tips

It is important that your students know the behavior expected of them while on a field trip. To ensure this, review field trip etiquette with your students several times before the trip.

• Listen and follow directions.

• Pay attention when someone is speaking.

• Avoid disturbing others. Keep your voice to a whisper.

• Always walk.

• Preserve natural areas by staying on paths or walkways.

- Handle only those displays that you are given permission to touch.
- Keep quiet during movies or presentations.
- Be polite. Raise your hand if you have a question.

Rule of Thumb

A good rule of thumb: Let your students know that their attitudes, behavior, and interest toward those they meet on their field trip reflect on the whole group and their learning environment. It is important that their conduct be guided by common sense and courtesy.

FIELD TRIP TIPS AND TRICKS

A field trip is an educationally recognized way to stimulate and complement students' interests and enrich their learning. However, unanticipated difficulties can thwart your best efforts and intentions. The suggestions below may help you head off difficulties.

- Enclose a cover letter with each permission slip. Tell the parents your learning goals, itinerary, costs (if their child is permitted spending money for snacks or the gift shop), mode of transportation, and any clothing considerations. Send out permission slips at least one week in advance. *Tip:* You will have a better return rate if you send them out at the beginning of a week.

Suggestions

- Make arrangements in advance for those students who do not bring back their permission slips and must stay behind. **Never take a child on a trip with only verbal authorization—always require written permission.**

- Include emergency medical information and release statements on your permission slips.

- Plan your travel route to the field trip site. Calculate and schedule your travel times and allow for delays en route. Provide your driver(s) with a copy of your route and travel time schedule. If you need lunch and a rest stop during travel, schedule them in your travel plans. If your trip requires leaving before or returning after regular hours, inform parents and remind them to make transportation plans for their children.

- Create an on-site trip timetable to keep you organized as you move through the day.

- Make identification tags for your students. Include the student's name, group name or school, and a contact name and phone number.

- Take group roll before you leave for the field trip site and again before you return to your learning environment.

- If your students are bringing sack lunches, prepare a container in which to transport them. Include garbage bags for cleanup. If you are stopping to eat at a restaurant, inform the management beforehand of your group size and expected arrival time.

- Prepare fun activities, such as games and songs, that your students can participate in as they travel.

- Plan for a shortfall in funding. Overestimate costs so that you may end up with a surplus rather than a shortage. Carry extra money with you for unexpected expenses.

- If possible, visit the site beforehand. Look for possible problem areas. Locate entrances, exits, and restrooms. Discuss the day's plan with an on-site representative and confirm the details of the trip.

- Carefully go over emergency procedures and safety issues with your students as a pre-trip activity. Review these with students just before leaving for the site.

- Prepare your chaperones. Give each a list of names of students in his or her group, a schedule, and a checklist of rules and procedures. *Tip:* Plan your adult-to-student ratio by age. *Example:* Each adult should have no more than five 5-year-olds, eight 8-year-olds, and so on.

- Assign students with behavioral problems to your group, or if their parents are chaperoning, to their parents' groups.

- Make a master field trip folder to take with you on the trip. Include a list of your students' names, addresses, and phone numbers, emergency information, permission slips, reservation forms, and confirmations.

- Be prepared to improvise. Go through the proposed trip in your mind, envisioning what may go wrong and what you could do in each event.

SAFETY-PROOFING YOUR FIELD TRIP

Safety is always a concern when dealing with students. Follow these suggestions to help safety-proof your trip.

Suggestions

- Organize an easy-to-carry first-aid kit to take with you on all field trips. Fill it with supplies you think may be helpful to have on hand. Do not forget to include important phone numbers. Be sure to let all your chaperones know where the kit will be located during the trip. Find out if any chaperone is trained in CPR. *Tip:* It is a good idea for anyone working with students on a daily basis to be trained in CPR.

- Put together an emergency "handy bag" that includes an extra pair of clothes for students who may not get to the bathroom on time or who get sick. Put in a washcloth, paper towels, an extra sack lunch or two, crackers (for travelers' upset stomachs), garbage bags, and anything else that might come in handy.

- Write trip safety procedures for your chaperones. Just before you leave, give them these reminders:

  Stay alert to the whereabouts and activities of the students in your group. "Count heads" frequently.

  Concentrate on the students in your care. Avoid being distracted by conversations with other adults.

Never leave the students alone or send them ahead of the group for any reason. Stay together at all times.

Supervise public bathrooms very carefully.

Make sure everyone uses the restroom before leaving on the trip and before leaving the trip site to return.

- Review all safety procedures with your students.

Rule of Thumb

A good rule of thumb: If an emergency occurs while you are on a field trip, remain calm. Your students will be looking to you for guidance and will model their behavior after yours.

PRE-TRIP ACTIVITIES

A field trip offers so much to see and learn! You can prepare students to focus on the purpose of the visit, arouse their curiosity, and provide the necessary background through a variety of pre-trip activities.

Suggestions

- Learn as much as you can about the trip site. Research library resources related to your destination. Send for brochures of the site and share them with your students.
- Show photographs of the trip site to your students.
- Teach your students vocabulary related to the subject.
  Example: observatory—telescope, constellation, light years, magnification.
- Create a bulletin board display to foster interest and curiosity about the upcoming trip.
- Visit the site beforehand (if at all possible) to familiarize yourself with the site and the route to the site. Purchase educational brochures that you can use in your teaching.
- Develop a brainstorming web with your students about the trip site and what they hope to see and learn.

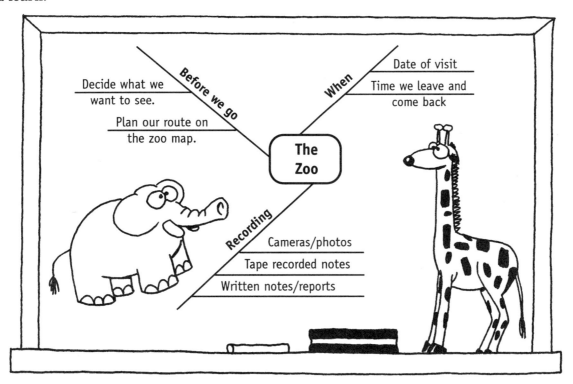

- Give multimedia presentations about the topic or field trip site. Use books, tapes, filmstrips, and videos.

- Create a "graffiti board" for your trip topic—a piece of poster board or a section of the chalkboard where your students can write questions they have about the topic or site.

- Invite a representative from the trip site to your learning environment to be a guest speaker prior to the trip.

- Help your students make a map of the route to the site.

- Have students create their own informational cover letter about the planned trip. This can be carried home or mailed to parents.

- Encourage each student to keep a "Journey Journal." This is a journal in which the student writes pre-trip thoughts and questions, observations and impressions during the trip, and follow-up activities after the trip. *Tip:* If you make several field trips during the year, have your students keep ongoing Journey Journals of all trips that year.

- Make sure your students understand what is required of them on the trip. Go over assignments in detail. Make a checklist for each student to take along with questions to answer or things to observe at the site.

- Plan reading, writing, science, social studies, or math activities around your field trip site or topic. *Examples:*

  Concert—Find out the four groups of instruments in an orchestra. Make a word search that includes at least three instruments from each group.

  Historical site (Gettysburg)—Pretend you fought in the battle of Gettysburg. Write a letter to President Lincoln explaining what happened.

  Telephone company—The telephone was invented by Alexander Graham Bell in 1876. How many years ago was that?

Rule of Thumb

A good rule of thumb: Logical thinking blossoms when students organize their own activities into workable sequences and set their own priorities and timetables.

TRIP ACTIVITIES

Your trip should be rewarding for you and your students! All your planning and pre-teaching should now result in a meaningful educational experience. Use the following activities to extend and reinforce your on-site visit:

Suggestions

- Provide opportunities throughout your visit for students to ask questions. Jot down questions that cannot be answered on the spot for discussion later.

- Instruct your students to take notes during their trip. Note taking can range from filling in a data sheet with information to recording in a Journey Journal. Later they can use the information to make a guidebook.

- Allow your students to take photographs throughout the visit (if appropriate). Check with the site representative to see if cameras and video equipment are allowed.

- A video of your trip and the "cast of characters" is a terrific way to bring the trip back to your learning environment again and again. Ask an adult to act as your trip media operator. Ask that person to make a tape recording or video of your trip. *Tip:* Your media operator should not have responsibility for a group of students.

- Pose questions at the site that require your students to use the facility to get the answers.
- Plan time at the conclusion of the visit for an on-site question-and-answer session. The tour guide can offer further explanations and clarifications.

Rule of Thumb

A good rule of thumb: Be alert to unplanned teaching opportunities during your field trip—a question, a comment, or an observation made by one of your students. These stimulate interest and create some of the best "teachable moments."

A good rule of thumb: Journal-keeping is an excellent tool for recording ideas, reflections, observations, and discoveries on any subject. Have your students keep a general journal as a way to encourage them to think of every day as an adventure worth capturing on paper.

JOURNEY JOURNALS

Journal writing involves reading, writing, and thinking—all essential elements of research. Instruct your students to research a topic related to their trip, then record in their journals what they have discovered. Assist young learners in keeping a Journey Journal that includes all trips they take and adventures they experience throughout the year. Keep the following points in mind:

Communication

- Instruct your students to write the following questions at the front of their journals to guide their writing: Who? What? When? How? Where? Why?
- Remind your students that a finished Journey Journal has all the elements of a book—complete with illustrations and a table of contents.
- Let students know that illustrations for Journey Journals can be drawings, but they also can be made by using cut-up brochures from the sites. Speech bubbles can be added to indicate comments.
- Stimulate your students to write by asking well-prepared questions that require them to think and express themselves independently.
- Develop vocabulary lists for your students to keep in their journals. This mini-dictionary will serve as a resource as the students record their impressions of a trip.
- Encourage your students to narrow their focus to one topic, learn as much as they can about it, then write about it in their journals. Suggest they begin with descriptive words, then expand their writing to include their feelings about a particular exhibit.

FIELD TRIP FOLLOW-UP ACTIVITIES

Suggestions

It is important for your students to share their field trip discoveries and to discuss thoroughly what they learned and how it relates to the ongoing study of a topic. Follow up your field trip with some of these activities:

- As soon as possible after you return from the trip, hold a brainstorming session. (Remember, brainstorming is a quick respond-and-record exercise without judgment or discussion.) Ask each student to contribute one comment, word, or observation about the trip and record these on the chalkboard or on a chart. Later, go back and discuss each item in more detail.

- Have your students write thank-you notes to everyone who assisted you during the trip. This will be a wonderful activity for your students, and the adults will welcome notes of appreciation. *Tip:* List the names of the on-site representatives, drivers, parents, chaperones, and so on. Ask pairs or small groups of students to select people and prepare cards or notes for them.

- Instruct the students to compose a "state of the trip" address to share with their parents. Have the students write their impressions of the trip as speeches, and then take them home and read then to their families.

- Let students visit other learning environments and give oral presentations of their impressions of the field trip. Be sure to tell them to include what they learned!

- Create a field trip topic learning center. Fill your center with reference materials, task cards, and books about the field trip topic. Challenge your students to reinforce and extend the knowledge they gained on the field trip by exploring a particular topic further.

- Keep a current collection of newspapers and news magazines for your students to skim through to find additional information on their field trip topic.

- Make a trip collage from the photographs taken on the trip. Ask your students to write about the collage.

- Document your trip on audiotape or videotape. Invite your students to record student-to-student interviews. Have students take the roles of reporter and site representative. The reporter interviews the "expert" from the field trip site. Remind your students to ask the following questions: Who? What? Where? When? Why? How?

- Instruct your students to invent and draw a symbol that could represent the field trip site. It could be a flag, logo, letterhead, doll, mug, T-shirt, etc.

- Tell your students to imagine that they are donating a large sum of money to the field trip site. Have them work in cooperative groups to decide how the money should be spent and why. Let each group share its thoughts.

- Show picture postcards and read the brief descriptions on the backs. Give each student a 5" x 8" (127 x 203 mm) blank index card on which to create a picture postcard of the field trip site.

- Instruct your students to write an advertisement enticing people to visit the field trip site.

- Ask your students to reflect on their field trip experience by writing a formal report. "Publish" the reports by compiling them into a book and putting it in your library.

- Ask your students to write a dialogue and music for a video, or captions for photos you took of the field trip site.

- Create a bulletin board about the field trip. Include photographs, drawings, and students' written work.

EVALUATING YOUR FIELD TRIP

Evaluation

The final step of the field trip experience is an honest appraisal of its educational value, including its strengths, weaknesses, and suggestions for improvement. The best way to judge the effectiveness of the experience is to base the evaluation on your reasons for taking the field trip. Here are some questions you may want to ask yourself: Did the trip accomplish its objectives? Were all the students' questions about the topic answered? Was additional information learned? Would I take this trip again? What could have been done differently to make this trip more successful? Survey your students, too. Are your impressions different from theirs?

Tip: Write up your evaluation and include it in your field trip folder. Share it with your students, the site representative, and parents. Honest evaluations lead to improved future trips.

Student Survey

Name _____ Date _____

Field Trip Site _____

The best thing about the trip was _____

_____

The worst thing about the trip was _____

_____

I saw _____ for the first time.

The most interesting thing was _____

_____

I think _____

was more interesting because we discussed it before the trip.

I would have liked to see _____

I think the trip was worthwhile/not worthwhile because

_____

FIELD TRIP SITE SUGGESTIONS

Suggestions

Extend your curriculum with a field trip! Here is a list of possible sites to consider:

- Airport
- Aquarium
- Arboretum
- Art gallery
- Bakery
- Concert
- Corporate facilities
- Courthouse
- Dentist's office

- Doctor's office
- Farmers' market
- Fast-food restaurant
- Fire department
- Florist
- Food-processing plant
- Geological site
- Government offices
- Grocery store
- Historical site
- Hospital
- Farm
- Library

- Military base
- Museum
- Newspaper
- Observatory
- Park
- Police department
- Post office
- Radio or Television station
- Telephone company
- Transit system
- Veterinarian's office
- Water treatment plant
- Weather station
- Zoo

FIELD TRIP CHECKLIST

Use this checklist as a guide to field trip planning. Adapt it to your specific needs, and have a great trip!

Steps to Take

Field Trip Checklist	✔
Determine the learning goals and objectives for the trip.	
Select the field trip site. Contact a site representative. Visit the site (if possible).	
Select a field trip date.	
Get all required approvals from your district (if applicable).	
Plan field trip funding.	
Arrange transportation.	
Inform parents and send permission slips. Include an emergency medical information form, phone numbers, and so on. Solicit chaperones.	
Prepare a "handy bag" and an emergency medical kit.	
Prepare a field trip folder. Include a roster of students, schedule, travel route, addresses, name tags, activities, and so on.	
Conduct pre-field trip instruction activities.	
Review rules, schedule of events, and activities to be completed at the site with the students. Make a checklist with the students.	
Follow up with post-field trip activities.	
Evaluate the field trip.	

Reproducible Form

Teaching Multicultural Awareness

Whether you are directly involved in a multicultural learning environment, or just interested in broadening your students' views, this chapter provides practical tips and steps to follow for teaching cultural awareness. The suggestions and activities provide opportunities for your students to explore multiculturalism close to home and around the world and to make your learning environment a place where all people, including those with different races, beliefs, cultures, or heritages, are respected and cherished.

DEVELOPING MULTICULTURAL AWARENESS

Awareness

Students who associate with others whose languages, religious practices, food preferences, skin colors, or even basic upbringings differ from their own learn to understand and appreciate cultural diversity. Such students develop a sense that, despite cultural differences, all people share the same basic needs and feelings. Begin to broaden your students' views with these activities:

Family Tree

Objective: To show that the concept and structure of "family" is influenced by one's culture.

1. Help your students draw their own family trees. (You may want to show them an example.)

2. Post the drawings in your learning environment for all students to examine.

3. Have students form small groups and discuss the family trees.

4. Lead a discussion with the whole group. Focus on questions like these:

   • When you think of family, whom do you include?

   • Where were your parents, grandparents, and great-grandparents born?

   • In what ways is your family like and different from other families? What special foods do you enjoy? What holidays do you celebrate? What activities do you do together?

   • What statements can you make about *all* families? *Some* families?

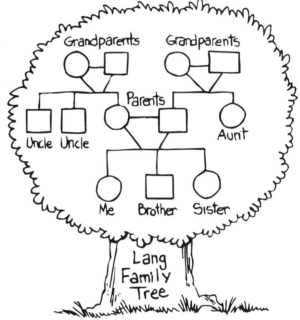

Who Lives in Our Country?

Objective: To show that your country is made up of people of diverse cultural backgrounds.

1. Post a large map of your country. Locate your state/province and talk about the people who live there.

2. Assign each student a state/province to research and find out about the population diversity there.

3. Have students talk about about their findings. What cultures are represented? Are any cultures particularly prevalent?

4. Initiate a discussion about the diversity of your country's population and the contributions of all people to the country.

What's in a Name?

Objective: To discover the origin of names and to foster pride in national heritage.

1. Challenge students to learn as much as they can about their names. Do their family names reflect particular nationalities? Do they denote a trade or craft? Have their family names been changed or abbreviated over time? Who chose their first names and why?

2. Ask your students to design family crests that reflect something they discovered about their names. Encourage them to share the designs with their families.

Let's Celebrate

Objective: To compare family traditions and celebrations.

1. Have students select an event celebrated in their households. Have children draw and write about what the celebrations entail—traditions, customs, foods, decorations, and so on.

2. Discuss and compare ways people celebrate. How are they similar? How are they different?

Participation

DISCOVERING OTHERS

Multicultural education should promote respect for all peoples, and should never set one group or culture above another. The ideal way for students to learn to appreciate diversity is through direct interaction. The following activities provide opportunities to learn about others firsthand.

Getting to Know You

Objective: To show students that much can be learned about another person without using language.

1. Assign partners. Tell students that they are to imagine that their partner does not speak their language.

2. Explain that their job is to find out as much as they can about their partner without using language (speaking or writing words). Suggest that they draw pictures or use gestures to communicate.

3. After students have had a chance to get to know another person nonverbally, let each pair share what they learned from the experience.

First Time

Objectives: To become aware that initial interactions can affect future perceptions. To identify actions and attitudes that are comforting to people in unfamiliar situations.

1. Ask your students to think about a time when they found themselves in an unfamiliar situation and were unsure what to do. (If you have students who immigrated from other countries, encourage them to share their experiences upon arrival.)

2. Ask your students to talk about how they felt in the situation. Were they scared? Did anyone offer to help them? How did they finally resolve the situation?

3. Talk about the feelings someone might have when coming to a new country. Discuss the fears that person might have and things that could be done to make the newcomer more comfortable.

Rule of Thumb

A good rule of thumb: Build multicultural participation by making it part of every subject you teach. Include aspects of different cultures in all the themes you study throughout the year. Be sure to highlight the cultures represented in your learning environment.

Country Talk

Objective: To increase awareness of and knowledge about the cultural heritages of students in the group.

1. Ask your students to identify their heritages. Place a large piece of paper on the wall for each country represented in the learning environment.

2. Have students move around the room, stopping at each country to write a question about the country or its people.

3. Instruct each individual or group representing a country to find the answers to the questions posed.

4. A few days later, hold a "country talk" in which the person or team shares what they learned about the country.

Guess Who?

Objective: To show that students of different cultures share many of the same interests.

1. Ask your students to complete these sentence starters:

> *My favorite place to be is . . .*
>
> *The thing I do best is . . .*
>
> *My favorite animal is . . .*
>
> *I am special because . . .*

2. Tell students not to put their names on the papers. Collect the papers, then pass out a paper to each student.

3. Instruct students to identify the mystery person by interviewing the others. They may ask questions like, "Is a treehouse your favorite place to be?"

Awareness

RESPECTING OTHER CULTURES

Bringing students of different cultural heritages together helps them better understand their own backgrounds and that of others. Your instructional program should guide students to regard all people without prejudice. Here are some multicultural activities to foster mutual respect:

Famous People Around the World

Objective: To establish that great men and women come from every culture.

1. Ask your librarian to help you select and gather a variety of biographies of famous people from different cultures.

2. Introduce each person to your students. Encourage each student to learn more about one of the people you introduced or another person.

3. Have each student thoroughly research his/her chosen person and report what was learned to the group.

Artifacts Adventure

Objective: To appreciate the significance of cultural artifacts.

1. Select a culture to highlight. Gather artifacts and pictures of significant cultural objects. You can borrow these items from families, libraries, and possibly museums.

2. Display the items unlabeled. Invite students to view the items as if they were a museum exhibit.

3. Ask students in pairs to choose an artifact to study. Have them find out what it is, how it is used, why it is important, and its significance to the culture. Have the students prepare index cards that identify the item and give information about it.

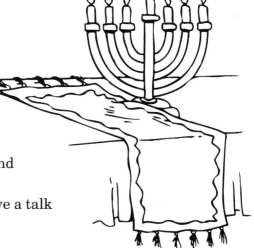

4. If possible, invite a person representing the culture to give a talk about the collection.

Great Guest Get-Togethers

Objective: To learn about another culture by listening to and talking with a guest.

1. Invite several guests to visit your learning environment throughout the year to share their knowledge of different cultures. These can be parents or grandparents of students, members of the community, or college professors or teachers.

2. Ask your guests to talk about such things as the customs, foods, crafts, music, and family life of a particular culture, plus anything personal including stories or items they would like to share.

3. Have your students write thank-you notes to the guests. This reinforces the positive power of acknowledgment.

Walk in My Shoes

Objective: To become aware of and express the feelings elicited by prejudice, isolation, or misunderstanding.

1. Prepare situations depicting prejudice, isolation, or misunderstanding. Ask students to put themselves in the situation and respond with a paragraph stating their feelings and reactions. Ask them to write about how they would feel and what they could do. Here are some examples:

   • You are not chosen for a team because of the color of your skin.

   • You are the only person in a group who does not speak the language. The others ignore you.

   • You enter a store and ask for something. The clerk laughs at you, then goes to tell his friend.

2. Hold a group discussion about students' responses.

Rule of Thumb

A good rule of thumb: An atmosphere of caring, trust, respect, and support helps build self-esteem. Students who feel good about themselves are better equipped to accept and appreciate differences in others.

YOUR ROLE AS AN EDUCATOR

Steps to Take

You are a role model for your students. Your day-to-day actions must match your words for a positive message to your students. Follow these steps:

1. Before choosing exactly how and what to teach your students, find out who they are through observation and conversation with them. Students' families are the best source of information about the students' skills, languages, values, and interests. Over time you will recognize individual strengths and weaknesses. Base your multicultural program on the needs of individual students and the group as a whole.

2. Make it a point to find information about the cultures and customs represented in your learning environment. *Example:* Hindu beliefs.

3. Be open-minded toward new materials and activities. Be willing to adapt ideas to your situation.

4. Establish an atmosphere of trust. Encourage your students to express their feelings. Be prepared to listen nonjudgmentally and to give positive guidance.

5. Demonstrate appropriate language and actions. Do not allow put-downs or mistreatment of anyone.

6. Pay attention to your students' nonverbal clues. Look for and act upon indications of discomfort.

7. Foster a cooperative learning environment in which everyone is both equally valued and responsible.

8. Establish a predictable routine in your learning environment. Knowing what to expect gives students a sense of security and assurance that everything is under control.

SELECTING MULTICULTURAL MATERIALS

Suggestions

The guidelines below are presented as questions to help you evaluate how well the multicultural materials and activities you are considering convey respect for your students, their families, and their cultural heritages. You may want to eliminate materials that do not meet one or more of these criteria.

- Are the people and cultures realistically and accurately portrayed? Is the material up-to-date?

- Are the students expected to learn primarily through extending their own experiences and gaining insight from one another?

- Is the material age-appropriate? Can your students understand and carry out most of the activities by themselves?

- Are common human characteristics portrayed, as well as a variety of differences among cultures?

- Is pride in cultural heritage fostered? Are historical references presented without bias? Are cultures celebrated?

- Is there an adherence to principles of respect for and equality among people of all races, nationalities, religions, sexes, and beliefs?

Rule of Thumb

A good rule of thumb: Use teaching materials and strategies that respect human diversity and equality. This is essential if your students are to become tolerant, fair-minded adults.

CONNECTING FAMILIES

Celebrate the cultural diversity of your students, their families, and your community with these activities:

- Conduct a "Parents' Night" meeting to discuss an overview of your plans to implement multicultural appreciation. Ask parents for their ideas as well.

- Seek out bilingual parents or community members to help you communicate with non-English-speaking parents.

Participation

- Send letters to families and community members asking them to participate in your multicultural program by sharing information or their talents with regard to cultural awareness. Contributions may include anything from ethnic cooking to a slide show of places they have visited.

- Hold a "Multicultural Game Night." Invite parents and community members into your learning environment to teach and play games popular in various cultures.

- Organize a "Multicultural Potluck Dinner." Ask families to prepare and bring a dish that reflects their heritage to share with everyone. *Tip:* You may want to ask a volunteer to collect and compile the recipes.

- Invite family members into your learning environment to share a craft or fine art activity with your students.

- Honor each family by sending a card for a holiday or celebration special to them. *Example:* Kwanzaa.

- Create a multicultural newspaper to share with families. Mention holidays, celebrations, and ongoing multicultural activities in your learning environment.

- Organize a multicultural fair. Each student or group of students presents to the guests a skit, demonstration, or project about something they learned that year. Let students decorate in multicultural themes. *Tip:* Holding a festive school-wide or organization-wide multicultural celebration is a great way to culminate the year!

A MULTICULTURAL LEARNING CENTER

Steps to Take

Devote part of your learning environment to the study of other cultures by setting up a multicultural learning center. The experience can be more valuable and personal if you involve the students in gathering materials and creating the center. Follow these steps:

1. Choose the focus of the unit or topic of study.

2. Decide what resources are needed. List books, tapes, films, and other audiovisual materials, plus possible sources of information from the community.

3. Invite your students to participate in collecting items that may be useful, such as clothing, post cards, currency, and photographs. Brainstorm possible ways to acquire materials—places to visit, people to contact, and so on.

4. At the center, provide construction materials with which your students may work—paper, pencils, markers, scissors, and so on.

5. Plan a variety of activities for the center. Make some activities easy and some challenging. The activities should involve listening, speaking, reading, and writing skills.

6. Include activities that span the curriculum, such as math, science, music, and art.

7. Make task cards for your learning center that list the materials and directions for each activity. *Tip:* You can have capable students compile information booklets on specific topics ahead of time for others to use at the center.

8. Include a pre-test and post-test activity so that you and your students can evaluate their performances.

9. Set up a schedule to help your students manage their time at the learning center. The schedule can be daily, weekly, or monthly. *Tip:* Use individual contracts to meet the needs and abilities of each student. *Example:* Joseph agrees to do one activity per week at the "Faces of Our Nation" learning center.

Rule of Thumb

A good rule of thumb: In general, learning centers are designed to be places where students learn and work independently, but you may want to guide your students in choosing activities and assess what they learn at your multicultural center.

Ideas for Learning Center Activities

Focus on Arts—Fill the center with reference materials on the arts and crafts of cultures and the traditions behind them. Provide materials for students to make their own versions of a particular craft. Instruct your learners that, before they make a craft, they must research its origin and significance. They must also be prepared to talk about their findings with the group. *Examples:* Indian totem poles, Mexican yarn art, Chinese writing, or African masks.

Current Events—Encourage your students to read about and become more aware of events happening outside their immediate circle. Assemble a collection of current newspapers and news magazines. Instruct students to read an article and answer a question about an event in another state/province or country, or a local event involving another cultural or ethnic group. Prepare a response sheet for the students.

MULTICULTURAL LANGUAGE ARTS

Suggestions

Enrich your students' language experiences by sharing the literature and language of a variety of cultures. Expand their horizons with these activities:

• Share stories and folktales of different cultures. This will foster critical thinking, enhance the process of seeing relationships, and help students make the connection between literature and themselves.

• Post a list of multicultural books selected especially for your students. Choose books that are relevant and on their enjoyment level.

• Create a small multicultural bulletin board. Each week post something different on the board and have students think, read, or write about it. *Examples:* a poem, picture, quote by a famous person, or clue to a mystery.

- Have your students choose a culture to research. Instruct them to investigate the language, family life, housing, work, clothing, foods, sports, arts, and music. Ask each student or team to report its findings, including the individual and group similarities and differences found within the culture.

- Talk with your students about cultural proverbs and family traditions. Choose a universal topic like birthdays, harvest festivals, or holidays. Chart the students' responses to show how different cultures express similar ideas.

- Invite your students to learn a few words in another language. Use bilingual parents or community members as "teachers," or find books that offer common words and pronunciations in different languages. Make flip-over flash cards to reinforce learning.

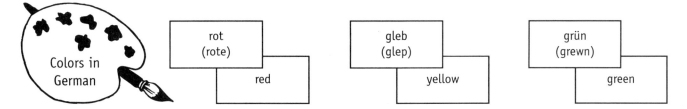

Rule of Thumb

A good rule of thumb: Select books to share with your students that are accurate and positive in their portrayal of cultural heritages and today's diverse families and workforce.

- Create a book about your learning environment that is a collection of photographs, brochures or souvenirs from field trips, and your students' stories and artwork relating to multicultural studies. Invite students to take the book home for an evening to share with their families.

- Help your students gain an understanding of the risks, adventures, and hardships faced by immigrants. Encourage students to reenact historical events as mini-plays. Give them sufficient background and tell them to strive for simplicity and authenticity.

- Instruct your students to report about a leader from their own or another culture. Tell them to investigate heroes and heroines, past and present, national and local. What qualities do these leaders exhibit? How do they help others? How can we follow their examples?

- Compare story characters with charts or diagrams. Comparisons can be made between two characters in a single story, or between characters in different stories. *Tip:* Encourage students to compare characters in stories from different cultures.

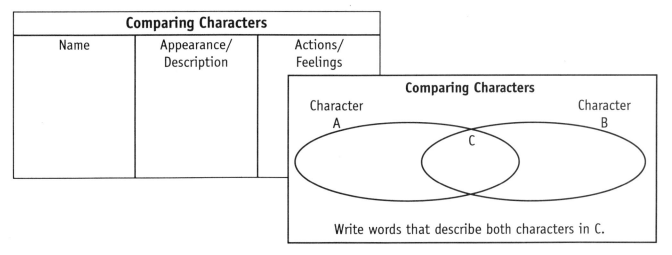

MULTICULTURAL MATHEMATICS

Suggestions

Numerals (number symbols) are a kind of universal language. Use these activities to connect cultures through mathematics.

- Activities that involve food are always popular and provide an excellent way to integrate math and language. Ask students to bring recipes for simple foods that represent their cultures. Have students make up math problems in which the recipe is used to find the solution. *Example:* How many cups of rice are needed to double the recipe for curried rice? If possible, make some of the foods with your students and enjoy them together.

- Challenge your students to learn the numbers from one to ten in another language. *Tip:* Use peer-teaching or provide books as resources.

- Take your students on a field trip to the grocery store. Instruct each student to pretend to purchase food for the family for one week on a $80.00 budget. Involve students in comparing and calculating prices and in exploring one another's food preferences.

- Have students make a bar graph of their extended families that show the number of people or their ages. (Extended families include parents, brothers, sisters, grandparents, aunts, uncles, and people who are meaningful to the students.)

Rule of Thumb

A good rule of thumb: Structure your learning environment so students have opportunities to work in pairs, on teams, and in committees to accomplish tasks and solve problems.

- Select a holiday or special day each month that is celebrated by a particular cultural or ethnic group. Create calendar word problems around that celebration. *Example:* Cinco de Mayo is May 5. Maria wants to make a piñata for her nephews. It will take her two weeks. On what day should she begin in order to have it done in time?

A good rule of thumb: Add special events of other cultures to your calendar, and build multicultural awareness at school and at home by studying and celebrating holidays from other cultures. Your students will benefit from learning many beautiful traditions.

- Tangrams are ancient Chinese puzzles. Pair students from different cultures to work on these tricky but fun puzzles. *Tip:* You can make your own tangram puzzle by drawing the arrangement shown on a cardboard square and cutting the pieces apart.

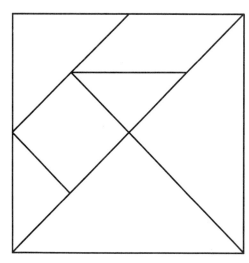

- Mosaics are found in cultures throughout the world. Provide examples of mosaics from different countries. Discuss the technique and the planning involved in creating a mosaic. Have each student plan a mosaic design, then use graph paper to color and cut out the squares needed to construct the final picture. Have the students paste the squares onto heavy paper to construct their mosaics.

Internet Information

Internet Terms

Acronym: A fast way of typing a phrase by using select letters from the phrase; an example is "HAND" for "Have A Nice Day"

Address: A location in cyberspace

Articles: Letters that are posted in newsgroups are referred to as articles; also referred to as "messages"

Baud: The speed at which modems transfer data

Bit: The smallest unit of information that can be sent among computers

Bookmark: Just like a regular bookmark that marks the page in a book, this marks your favorite web site right in your browser for easy retrieval.

Bounce: When your e-mail cannot get to where you tried to send it, it "bounces" back to your computer.

Browser: A program that allows you to look at web sites on the Internet

Bulletin Board Systems (BBS): Networks that your computer can dial into through your modem

Chat: Talking to someone on the computer by typing words on the computer keyboard

Cyberspace: The on-line world—this includes the Internet and the World Wide Web.

Data: Information that has been formatted so that it can be understood by a computer

Databases: Electronic file cabinets storing information in a specific category; for example, a school's database might contain information on all the students attending that school.

Directory: The information stored on your computer is divided into sections known as directories. Each directory can contain different files.

Documents: Computer documents may contain text, pictures, maps, or video clips.

Domain name: The name given to a host computer on the Internet

Dot: What you say instead of "period" when you are talking about Internet addresses. For example, "myname.com" would be said "my name dot com"

Download: Getting information from the Internet to your computer; once you download a file, it will be stored on your computer for retrieval whenever you want.

E-mail: Electronic mail

FAQ: Frequently Asked Questions; most newsgroups and mailing lists have FAQ files which answer basic questions for newcomers.

File: A "folder" on your computer, like a folder in a filing cabinet, which holds information programs, documents, pictures, etc.

Flaming: Unreasonably criticizing someone in cyberspace

Freeware: Software you can download and use without paying for it

Gateway: A computer system that acts as a translator for different types of computers to allow them to interact in cyberspace

Highlighted: A word or phrase marked so that it stands out, usually by a different colored text or by underlining; in cyberspace, these are usually hyperlinks that can take you to other locations.

Hotlist: The same as a bookmark

HyperText Markup Language (HTML): The programming language a computer uses to create web pages

Icon: A picture that you click on with your mouse in order to open up another page

Internet: International Network of smaller computer networks; contains the World Wide Web

Links: Same as hypertext but can also include images, that if clicked on, will take you to another location in cyberspace

Listserv: A listserv is a program that sends and receives e-mail to a group of subscribers.

Lurking: Visiting newsgroups on the Internet without posting messages

Mailing List: Like a subscription to an on-line magazine, this lets you sign up to receive articles and e-mails automatically.

Modem: Shorthand for Modulator-Demodulator; a piece of equipment that lets your computer talk to other computers and hook into the Internet over telephone lines

Net: Short for Internet

Netiquette: On-line manners; the proper way to behave while you're surfing the Internet

Network: A group of computers joined together to form one big computer by data-carrying links

Newsgroups: Sites on the Internet at which you can discuss almost any subject you can imagine; there are currently close to 17,000 active newsgroups.

On-line: When your computer is connected to another machine via modem or cable, you are on-line.

Page: A document on the Internet is often referred to as a "page" or a "home page." This is what you see when you visit a web site.

Password: A secret word you type into the computer for access to certain web sites

Posting: Sending an e-mail message to a mailing list or a newsgroup

Public Domain Software: Like freeware but it's not copyrighted, so it can be modifed, copied, or distributed.

Search Engines: Web sites that go on the Internet and search for information for you

Service Provider: An organization that provides access to the Internet

Shareware: Software that you can download and "try out" before paying for it

Site: The physical location of a computer or its location in cyberspace; also known as web site

Snail Mail: Mail sent the old-fashioned way, through the postal service; slow compared to e-mail

SPAM: Sending Particularly Annoying Messages; this is the electronic equivalent of junk mail.

Subject Line: A title for your e-mail message so the recipient knows what the e-mail is about

Surfing: Following links from one web site to another, like riding one wave after another when surfing

Telnet: The network terminal protocol that allows you to log onto any other computer on the network

Threads: Discussions within a discussion found on newsgroups or mailing lists

URL: Universal Resource Locator; the address for any type of web site or Internet resource

Usenet: The collective term for newsgroups or discussion groups

User Name: The name you use to log on to the network

Virus: A destructive program that hides in files that you download from the Internet or receive from floppy disks

Web Browsers: Programs that navigate you through the World Wide Web

World Wide Web (WWW): The network of computers that forms the on-line world; a part of the Internet

All About Site Addresses

What Is a URL?

URL stands for Universal Resource Locator. It is a key to getting where you want to go on the Internet. This is what a typical URL looks like: http://www.thisplace.com

http://www.

http://www. means "HyperText Transport Protocol://World Wide Web." It is a shorthand term to describe the way the Web moves information throughout the networks and around the world. These can be:

www	located on the World Wide Web
gopher	located on a Gopher server
news	located on a Usenet news group
ftp	located on an FTP server

Next, comes the name of the site you want to visit, such as "thisplace." This tells the Internet the exact page you want. And, finally, comes the domain name, which gives you a clue as to what type of organization it is:

edu	U.S. educational institution
com	commercial organization
org	non-profit organization
gov	government organization

URL Problems

The most common reason for a URL to fail is a typo. Look closely and see if anything is misspelled. A URL cannot contain blank spaces. URLs are case sensitive, so make sure that you correctly type the letters that are supposed to be capitalized and the letters that are supposed to be lowercase. The URL should end either with a domain name or with a file name.

It is common to receive the error message "404, File Not Found." This means the web server could not find a file matching that URL. Make sure you typed the URL correctly. Try again later—the file could be a popular site and you are getting a "busy signal." But it could also mean that this URL does not even exist anymore.

On-Line Safety Rules for Kids

1. Do not give out any personal information such as your address, telephone number, or parents' places of work.
2. Do not give out the addresses, telephone numbers, or names of your school or after-school activities.
3. Tell your parents or teacher immediately if you see anything or anyone that makes you feel uncomfortable.
4. Never agree to get together with someone you meet on-line without first checking with your parents.
5. Never send a person your picture or anything else personal without first checking with your parents.
6. Do not respond to any messages that are mean or that in any way make you feel uncomfortable. Tell your parents or teacher right away so that it can be reported to the on-line service.
7. Set up rules with your parents for going on-line at home. Decide upon the time of day to be on-line, the length of time to be on-line, and appropriate areas to visit.
8. Do not access other areas or break these rules without permission.

Web Sites

Animals

Animal Connection
http://www.cyberark.com/
At The Farm
http://miksike.com/unit/
Big Cats On-line
http://dialspace.dial.pipex.com/agarman/
Birch Aquarium at Scripps Introduction Page
http://aqua.ucsd.edu/
Bugs in the News!
http://falcon.cc.ukans.edu/~jbrown/bugs.html
Cats! Wild to Mild
http://www.lam.mus.ca.us/cats/
Crocodiles
http://www.pbs.org/wgbh/nova/crocs/
Dinosaur Reference Center
http://www.crl.com/~sarima/dinosaurs/
Dogz and Catz
http://www.dogz.com/
Download-a-Dinosaur
http://www.rain.org/~philfear/download-a
   dinosaur.html
Endangered Species
http://www.nceet.snre.umich.edu/EndSpp/
   Endangered.html
Gorilla Foundation Homepage
http://www.gorilla.org/index.html
Horsefun Home Page
http://www.horsefun.com/
National Zoo Home Page
http://www.si.edu/natzoo/
Rattlesnake Ranch
http://www.wf.net/~snake/index.html
Shark!
http://www.goodtech.co.uk/shark/
Sounds of the World's Animals
http://www.georgetown.edu/cball/animals/animals.html
WWF for Kids
http://www.wwfcanada.org/wwfkids/index.html
Welcome to Healthy Pets
http://www.healthypet.com/index.html

Food & Nutrition

Cooking with Kids
http://www.lightcooking.com/kids.html
Fitness Files Home Pages
http://fyiowa.webpoint.com/fitness/
Nutrition Cafe
http://exhibits.pacsci.org/nutrition/
Shape Up, America
http://www.shapeup.org/sua/
The Story of Milk
http://moomilk.com/tours/tour1-0.htm

Fun & Games

All Magic Guide
http://www.uelectric.com/allmagicguide.html
For Kids Only+
http://www.ci.berkeley.ca.us/bpl/kids/index.html
The Fun Centre!
http://www.interlog.com/~brucem/funcntr.html
Games
http://www.cyberteens.com/games/Games.html
Kids Love A Mystery
http://www.kidsloveamystery.com/
Walt Disney Pictures
http://www.disney.com/DisneyPictures/index.html
Warner Bros. Home Page
http://www.warnerbros.com

History

Black History
http://www.kn.pacbell.com/wired/BHM/hunt.html
Castles on the Web
http://fox.nstn.ca/~tmonk/castle/castle.html
Constitution of the United States
http://www.law.emory.edu/FEDERAL/usconst.html
Explorers of the World
http://www.bham.wednet.edu/explore.html
4000 Years of Women in Science
http://www.astr.ua.edu/4000WS/4000WS.html
Grolier Online's The American Presidency
http://www.grolier.com/presidents/preshome.html
Mysterious Mummies
http://www.pbs.org/wgbh/nova/chinamum/
The Original Titanic Page
http://gil.ipswichcity.qld.gov.au/~dalgarry
The TimeTraveller
http://armadillo.co.za/TimeTraveller/
The Underground Railroad
http://www.cr.nps.gov/delta/under.htm

Human Body

Anatomy
http://rpisun1.mda.uth.tmc.edu/se/anatomy
Anatomy of the Eye
http://www.eyenet.org/public/anatomy/anatomy.html
Body Atlas
http://www.bluecares.com/good/body/
The Heart: An Online Exploration
http://sln.fi.edu/biosci/heart.html
How Your Brain Really Works
http://quest.arc.nasa.gov/neuron/events/baw/
Human Anatomy On-line - InnerBody.com
http://www.innerbody.com/indexbody.html

Math

Mathemagic Activities
http://www.scri.fsu.edu/~dennisl/CMS/activity/
  math_magic.html
Money Curriculum Unit
http://woodrow.mpls.frb.fed.us/econed/curric/money.html
Statistics Every Writer Should Know
http://nilesonline.com/stats/
Willoughby Home
http://Schoolcentral.com/Willoughby/default.htm

Planet Earth

All About Rainbows
http://www.unidata.ucar.edu/staff/blynds/rnbw.html
Desert Life in America's Southwest
http://www.desertusa.com/life.html
Give Water A Hand
http://www.uwex.edu/erc/
Glacier
http://www.glacier.rice.edu/
Global Warming: Focus on the Future
http://www.envirolink.org/orgs/edf/
Meteorology A to Z
http://www.nwlink.com/~wxdude/topics.html
National EarthQuake Information Center
http://gldss7.cr.usgs.gov
Rainforest Tour
http://www.pbs.org/tal/costa_rica/rainwalk.html
Volcano World
http://volcano.und.nodak.edu/vw.html
The Wonderful World of Trees
http://www.domtar.com/arbre/english/

Science

Attack of the Killer Germs
http://tqd.advanced.org/3361/
Ask Dr. Science
http://www.drscience.com/
Children, Science for Kids,
Projects & Experiments
http://www.waterw.com/~science/kids.html
Faster Than Sound
http://www.pbs.org/wgbh/nova/barrier/
How Light Works
http://pen1.pen.k12.va.us:80/Anthology/Div/Albemarle/
  Schools/MurrayElem/InstructionalResources/Light/
  How_Light_Works.html
I Want To Be A Veterinarian
http://vet.futurescan.com/vet/index.html
The MAD Scientist Network
http://medinfo.wustl.edu/~ysp/MSN/
Mr. Warner's Cool Science!
http://home.unicom.net/~warnerr/
NPR Science Friday Kids Connection
http://www.npr.org/programs/sfkids/

Nature and Science

http://www.microweb.com/nature/index.html
Nova Online: Kaboom!
http://www.pbs.org/wgbh/nova/kaboom/
Science Daily
http://www.sciencedaily.com/index.htm
Strange Science
http://www.turnpike.net/~mscott/index.htm
The Wizards Lab
http://library.advanced.org/11924/index.html
The World of Benjamin Franklin
http://sln.fi.edu/franklin/rotten.html

Social Studies

CircusWeb! Circus Present and Past
http://www.circusweb.com/circuswebFrames.html
Future Culture
http://www.wcpworld.com:80/future/culture.htm
The Great American Web Site
http://www.uncle-sam.com/
Kids Farm
http://www.kidsfarm.com/
Native American Home Pages
http://www.pitt.edu/~lmitten/indians.html
Pony Express
http://www.databahn.net/library/inet/history/pony/
  index.htm

Space

Apollo 11
http://nssdc.gsfc.nasa.gov/planetary/lunar/apollo11.html
Ask An Astronaut
http://www.nss.org/askastro/home.html
Astronomy For Kids
http://www.frontiernet.net/~kidpower/astronomy.html
Basics of Space Flight
http://www.jpl.nasa.gov/basics/
Kennedy Space Center
http://www.spaceportusa.com/
NASA K-12 Internet: LFS On-line
http://quest.arc.nasa.gov/lfs/lfsnew.html
The Nine Planets
http://seds.lpl.arizona.edu/nineplanets/nineplanets/
  nineplanets.html
Stars and Constellations
http://www.astro.wisc.edu/~dolan/constellations/
The Sun: A Multimedia Tour
http://www.astro.uva.nl/michielb/od95/

Sports

AllSports Sports Central
http://www.allsports.com/allsport.htm
Ancient Olympics
http://olympics.tufts.edu/
A Great Physical Education Site
http://educ.ubc.ca/dept/cust/pe/